ADVENTURES UNDER FIRE!

World War II Memoirs and
50-Mission Diary
Aboard the B-17 Flying Fortress
1942 to 1945

15th AF   416 SQD

Albert C. Henke

ISBN: 978-1-58597-418-4

Library of Congress Control Number: 2006925940

LEATHERS
PUBLISHING
4500 College Boulevard
Overland Park, Kansas 66211
888-888-7696
www.leatherspublishing.com

Acknowledgments

It is with great respect and honor that I dedicate this book to the men with whom I flew during World War II, especially the members of the crew of the B-17 Robert E. Lee. Without their bravery, dedication, hard work, and sense of humor, this book would not have been possible.

Front row (left to right): Lieutenant Ervin Haron, Navigator; Lieutenant Don Hemmingson, Bombardier; Captain Burnham Shaw, Co-Pilot; Major David MacDonald, Pilot-Squadron Commanding Officer

Back row (left to right): Staff Sergeant Clarence Danielson, Left-Waist Gunner; Staff Sergeant Phillip Wojack, Ball Turret Gunner; Technical Sergeant Ross McKinney, Radio Operator/Gunner; Staff Sergeant Howard Carter, Right-Waist Gunner; Staff Sergeant Al Henke, Tail Gunner; Technical Sergeant Gene Canciglia, Flight Engineer/Gunner

Although my diary that makes up most of this book was written at the time of the War, as I write this, I am 87 years old. Many of the men mentioned have passed away. Through the years, I have treasured their friendship and feel honored to have served with them.

Someone else, whom I must mention, is the guy who was like a brother to me, Staff Sergeant Daniel Ives. Throughout most of my Air Force career, Dan and I were together. Although we were not assigned to the same crew, most of our missions were to the same target. During the period before we were assigned to a crew, we flew several missions on the same plane. I first met Dan when we enlisted at Fort Leavenworth, Kansas. We took all of our training together, went overseas together, started our missions on the same plane, on the same day, and finished our missions within a week of each other. We were sent back to the States at the same time. We were on different ships, but in the same convoy. After receiving a furlough, we were both sent to Miami, Florida, for a rest. The first day in Miami, I could not believe it when I saw Dan walking down the beach toward me. We spent three weeks in Miami and then didn't see each other until the War was over.

Although there were many hardships to endure during our service in World War II, there were also some friends who I will always cherish. One of these friends is Vernon "Bud" Wells. Wells and I took all of our training together. When it was time for us to go overseas, Wells was sent to the 8th Air Force in England, and I was assigned to the 12th Air Force and, later, the 15th Air Force in North Africa. We kept in touch with each other during and after the War. Wells went to college after the War and became a mechanical engineer. He worked for U.S. Steel in the Chicago area. Much of his career was spent building back the steel mills in Germany that our bombs destroyed during World War II. Wells lives in St. John, Indiana, not far from where our oldest daughter, Nancy, lives in Munster, Indiana, so we have kept in contact with him and his wife, Doris. Nancy refers to Wells as her, "Dad away from home." If she needs advice, or help with her car or house, he is right there for her.

I want to thank my wife of 60 years, Mary, and my children, Nancy, Marsha, Don, and Sharon. They have urged me to write this book and have helped by editing, proofreading, and keeping Mary on track with the computer by scanning photos and coordinating files.

In addition, I would like to express my gratitude to some friends, Technical Sergeant Wallace Bush and Lieutenant George Perry from the 99th Bomb Group Historical Society. They planted the seed that started me on the path to write this book and gave me the encouragement to get on with it. George also has written a book, *For You Der Var Iss Ofer*. Unfortunately, Wally did not write a book, but he should have. I have a collection of many letters Wally wrote to me through the years that should be in the hands of historians.

Thanks also goes to Sister Phyllis Dye, O.S.B. Sister Phyllis was my daughter Nancy's sixth grade teacher. While studying the history of World War II, Nancy took my 50-mission diary to school for one of her class projects. After reading my diary, Sister Phyllis suggested that I should put it in a book. Sister Phyllis is retired from teaching now, but is still a professional at motivating people to reach their goals.

So here I am after all of these years, "putting it in a book!"

Albert C. Henke

Special Thanks

I wish to extend special thanks for photos, illustrations, and information to the following people:

Bill Canciglia
Joe Canciglia
Burnham E. Shaw, Jr.
Wiley Shaw
Vernon Wells

I also wish to extend special thanks to the following people who reviewed this book before publication:

Dave Blake
Joe Daniels
Marilyn Daniels
Clarice Hahn
Arlene Levin
Henry Levin
Sandra Saberniak
Darrell Simons

Introduction

    This book is based on a 50-mission diary kept throughout my tour overseas during World War II. The diary was written approximately five hours after the completion of each mission. It is a first-hand account of some of my actual experiences. Additional details included in this book come from letters I wrote home to my mother in Kansas City, Missouri. She kept those letters, and later gave them to me. The letters are also first-hand accounts of my World War II experiences.

    I served in both the 12th Air Force and the 15th Air Force. The 15th Air Force was activated in October, 1943, about a month after I arrived in North Africa. Of the 50 missions I flew, 14 were from Tunis, North Africa. The last 36 were from our base at Foggia, Italy. I was assigned to the 99th Bomb Group, 416th Squadron, as a tail gunner on a B-17 Flying Fortress. My first mission was September 16, 1943. My last mission was seven months later, on April 2, 1944.

    In the early part of the War, the American Air Force had many losses. The loss of planes and crews was extremely high. (During one six-day period in 1944, over 225 heavy U.S. bombers were lost.) Airmen faced many dangers besides the German fighters and flak. The bombers did not have pressurized cabins so demand-type oxygen masks had to be worn while flying at high altitude. If the oxygen mask malfunctioned or became unplugged, it could cause death in about three minutes. There was no way of heating the planes, and at high altitude, the temperature reached 65 degrees below zero or lower. We wore heat suits that were plugged into the electrical system. We also wore heavy gloves and boots that were plugged into the suit. I once read that in 1943, one in three tail gunners was killed, and they just washed the blood out the tail and threw another gunner in. I cannot verify the accuracy of this statement, but it sounds pretty accurate to me.

    The 15th Air Force required airmen to fly 50 missions before being rotated back to the States for reassignment. Toward the end of my tour overseas, we received credit for two missions if we flew a combined raid with the 8th Air Force. However, there were other times that we flew and were not credited for the mission because the target was obscured by clouds that prevented us from dropping the bombs. (This explains why there are a few discrepancies between diary entries and the verified mission logs.)

When we were flying out of Tunis, North Africa, the majority of our missions were very long. The longest mission I flew was 11 hours and 20 minutes. The target was a German Messerschmitt aircraft factory located at Wiener Neustadt, Austria. Our planes had to land at Gela, Sicily, on the way home to refuel. This landing strip was built for fighter planes and was not intended for planes as large as the B-17 Flying Fortress. On these deep penetration missions, we did not have the luxury of fighter escorts because they did not have enough fuel to fly that far. At this time, they did not have the capabilities of refueling a plane in the air as they do today.

Of my missions, I flew 33 in the tail-position, with 30 of these in the lead ship. I had a panoramic view of complete plane formation, and one of my duties was to report to our pilot any plane that had to drop out, so that he could notify Air/Sea rescue. At the briefings before each mission, I received a list of the planes on that mission that indicated the number and position of each plane.

While flying on these 50 missions, I actually witnessed 55 direct hits in which the bomber, still loaded with bombs and fuel, exploded into a ball of fire, blowing the plane and the 10- or 11-man crew into bits. Other planes with engines on fire, or sometimes with a wing or tail blown off, often left our formation. Some of these men were able to parachute safely from the plane, only to take their chances in enemy territory. Depending on where they had to bail out, they were either picked up by the Germans and taken prisoners, or some were lucky enough to be met by members of the underground who helped them to escape back to the American lines. Some of the planes that returned to our base were so severely damaged, it was a miracle they were able to stay in the air.

It is my intent that this book will serve as a historical record. I hope, in some way, this will attest to the bravery of the crews and the danger we faced.

Table of Contents

Chapter

The Early Years

December 7, 1941, the day the Japanese bombed Pearl Harbor, was a day every American living at that time will always remember. This day changed the lives of all Americans, and my family was no exception. My family's experiences before World War II, however, were typical of many American housholds.

I was born July 1, 1920, on a farm about five miles northeast of Brunswick, Missouri. My family consisted of my mother, Mary Rose Unternaehrer Henke; my father, Ernest Charles Henke; an older brother, Harold Henke; a younger sister, Juanita Voncele Henke (known as Bonnie); and myself, Albert Henke. Our family moved to Ranger, Texas, when I was less than a year old. The Texas "Oil Boom" was in full swing, and people were flocking there to seek their fortunes. Papa loved adventure and was excited about pulling up stakes and going to Texas. I'm not so sure Mom was as excited as he was about the move, but she went along with his wishes.

Papa operated a garage and gas station on the main street of Ranger, Texas. My mother ran a boarding house for some of the oil workers. In 1926, Papa accepted a job as a mechanic for Black, Sivelson, and Bryson Tank Company, and we moved to Borger, Texas. Borger was a boomtown located about 38 miles north of Amarillo in the panhandle of Texas. The town was not quite a year old. When I was about five years old, the oil boom started at Borger, Texas. More than 3,000 people converged on this town, which was not ready for such an influx of people. Borger had the reputation of being a truly wild town, and the Texas Rangers moved in to try to restore law and order. Papa moved to Borger before we did. After about a month, when he was settled, he sent word for us to join him. Mom, Harold, and I boarded a train for Panhandle, Texas, which was about 50 miles southeast of Borger. We arrived about 6:00 p.m. one evening. The Panhandle depot was an old railroad boxcar sitting on the bank within 10 feet of the tracks. This was about two miles from the main part of town. Our lodging that night was in a tent with a wood floor and no lights. The restroom facility was an outside one-hole toilet.

Papa drove down to pick us up. There were no roads leading to Borger, just trails across the prairie. A person could see for miles across that prairie. It was flat, with very few trees, and hundreds of tumble weeds blowing in every direction. We lived in a tent until the oil company could build a house for us. The oil companies furnished housing for their employees.

On January 5, 1928, my younger sister was born. I was seven years old when Bonnie was born. A couple of my pals, Bernie Butler and George Cook, and I were discussing who brought babies. Bernie said his mom said a stork brought him, but I set him straight right quick. I told him, "A stork didn't bring my little sister. The doctor brought her in a little black bag!"

I started first grade in Borger in a brand-new all-brick school. (It was still in use as a trade/technical school, at the time of our visit in 1986, on the occasion of the town's 60th anniversary celebration. During our visit, I donated my first grade perfect attendance certificate to the Borger Museum, which is on display there. We also donated a 10x42-inch panoramic picture of Borger's main street taken in 1927, the first birthday of the town. The picture showed 55 wooden oil derricks in the downtown area. Main Street was three miles long.)

Shortly after Bonnie's birth, Papa took a job as a mechanic with Marland Oil Company. The company's home base was in Ponca City,

Oklahoma, so we were on the move again. Ponca City was a nice, modern town. Marland Oil Company was the largest employer in Ponca City.

Papa really enjoyed working for the Marland Oil Company. He had a great respect for Mr. Marland because he treated his employees well. Our house in Ponca City was a nice, modern house (inside plumbing). It was a sad day for the employees of Marland Oil Company in 1929 when the stock market crashed. Mr. Marland lost his company to the New York bankers, and it became the Conoco Oil Company. Papa lost his job. We loaded as many of our possessions as possible (including Mom's Singer sewing machine) into a trailer that Papa pulled with his 1926 Model-T Ford coach and headed for Kansas City, Missouri.

During the Great Depression, it was next to impossible to find a job. Papa was lucky to find employment with a bus company. I do not remember the name of the company, but it was located in the Turner district of Kansas City, Kansas. It was there, on the night of January 16, 1936, while working alone, that Papa was overcome by carbon monoxide and lost his life. (There were no modern ventilating systems at that time.)

After moving to Kansas City, Harold and I both spent our summers working on our uncles' farms in Brunswick, Missouri. They each owned half of my Grandfather Unternaehrer's farm. Frank and Barbara Unternaehrer, my mother's parents, bought this 160-acre farm in 1910. Frank, Adolph, and Albert built a beautiful two-story, three-gable farmhouse on the northeast corner of the farm. It was the showplace of the neighborhood. When Frank died, Adolph and Albert each bought half of the farm from the estate. Uncle Adolph owned the half on which the home stood.

From 1930 through 1934, during my summer vacations, I stayed with Uncle Adolph, and my cousins, Rosetta and Udell. Aunt Hattie, Uncle Adolph's wife, died a few years earlier. Harold stayed next door with Uncle Albert and Aunt Grace.

ADVENTURES UNDER FIRE!

I was 10 years old when I first stayed on the farm. Even at that age, I learned to work hard and long hours. Our uncles and their families were very good to us, and we learned so much during our time there. I was driving cars and tractors, and plowing with Uncle Adolph's huge 1,800-pound mules, Pete and Jerry. I was allowed to drive the car to the city limits of Brunswick. This was not something I would get to do in the city. The first year I was there, Uncle Adolph bought a new 1930 Ford Coach. That first Saturday night after he bought it, we all got ready to go to town. I just kind of hung back because I just knew he would never allow me to drive his new car. When he came out, he climbed in the back seat so I knew I was going to get to drive. Wow! I had to sit on a pillow to see out of the windshield, but that day I felt that I was 10 feet tall. Farm work in the 1930s was hard, but those years were some of the most fun years of my life.

In Kansas City, we attended Benjamin Harrison Grade School. One of our teachers was Miss Ethel Noland. Miss Noland was an excellent, dedicated teacher who took a great interest in her students. Her cousin was Harry S. Truman. She spoke about her cousin, Harry, many times and said someday he would be a very important person. At this time, Harry was the Circuit Judge for Jackson County, Missouri.

Harold was an avid student and had a great love for history. Miss Noland encouraged him to keep his grades up when he went to Northeast High School. She told him she would use her influence with Cousin Harry, who by this time was a Congressman from our district, to recommend him for an appointment to West Point. This was Harold's ambition throughout high school.

Papa was 41 years old when he died in 1936. Harold was 17 and had completed half of his junior year. I was 15 and a freshman. Bonnie was eight years old and in the lower grades. Other than a small insurance policy that my Papa had, there was no other income, such as Social Security or welfare. Mom made a meager salary cleaning houses and doing ironing for people. Harold and I both worked in the NYA (National Youth Association) program at school and each earned $3.00 a week. We were able to get by financially by pooling all of our resources.

Harold's dream of going to West Point, however, went down the drain. After Harold graduated, a friend of my mother knew a lady, Elmira Collins, who worked in the personnel department at Western Auto Supply Company. It was through her influence that Harold was able to get hired at Western Auto's home office in Kansas City, Missouri. In 1937, you had to know someone in a company in order to get hired. In 1939, when I graduated, Harold was able to get me on at Western Auto also. With Harold and I working, our financial situation improved. In fact, it improved so much that we decided to buy a 1936 Chevrolet together. We rode to work together and took a few riders whose fees helped us with the car payments and expenses. By early 1941, the Chevrolet was paid for, so we decided to buy a 1940 Pontiac. I really thought I had arrived when I became half-owner of such a nice car.

My family (left to right) Charlie, Albert, Harold, and Mary Henke in Ranger, Texas, 1923.

The boomtown of Borger, Texas.

ADVENTURES UNDER FIRE!

Childhood friends (left to right) Bernie Butler, Queenie (dog), Albert Henke, and George Cook playing on the back porch while awaiting the birth of Al's younger sister, Bonnie.

Frank and Adolph Unternaehrer standing on the front porch of the Unternaehrer home in Brunswick, Missouri.

The home office of the Western Auto Supply Company, Kansas City, Missouri, where I spent 60 years of employment. I was involved in the purchase of the landmark circle arrow sign atop the building.

I'm standing next to the "pride and joy" of Harold and Albert Henke—the 1940 Pontiac we purchased together.

Chapter

"You're in the Army Now...
You Can Gripe All You Want,
But It Won't Do You Any Good!"

When the United States entered World War II in December of 1941, my brother, Harold, was of draft age. He knew it would just be a matter of time before he would be drafted. The week after Pearl Harbor, he enlisted in the Signal Corp. In 1942, he applied for O.C.S. (Officer Candidate School) and graduated as a 2nd Lieutenant assigned to the Air Force. One of his classmates in O.C.S was the Oscar-winning movie star, Clark Gable.

Everyone I knew was leaving for some branch of the service, and I was really getting anxious to join, too. I would not be of draft age until the summer of 1942. There were still a few payments due on the Pontiac, so I felt an obligation to remain home until the car was paid off.

When I felt my family's financial situation had become stable, I thought I should serve my country. It was a difficult decision to join the service, which meant leaving Mom and my sister, Bonnie, to fend for themselves. At this time, Mom owned and operated a small neighborhood café. She made chili, hamburgers, and homemade pies. Bonnie, now a teenager, helped her after school and in the summer. I could have possibly received a deferment from the draft because I was the sole male provider of our household. Mom said she thought I should join so I could get into the Air Force. Harold and I thought, with the income she received from the café, and that if we each sent home some money each month, she and Bonnie would be able to survive financially.

A cousin, Roy Bates, who lived in Herrington, Kansas, and I were both in the same situation. He, too, was expecting a draft notice any day. There was a short period of time between the first draft notice and the final draft notice during which a person could opt to enlist into the branch of service he wanted. Otherwise, he had no choice. The two of us made a pact that whenever either of us received a first-draft notice, we both would enlist the next day. Roy also wanted to go into the Air Force's pilot training program. We thought that if we enlisted together, there might be a chance that we would stay together. Roy received his draft notice in October, 1942, so we both enlisted in the Air Force as planned. We discussed with the recruiting officer what our chances were of staying together. He was certain this would be no problem.

Roy's physical showed that he had color blindness, so he was ineligible for pilot training. We then agreed to sign up for airplane mechanic school. The recruiter gave us each a letter. He said, "In the event that you are not accepted for mechanic school or if they try to split you up, just take this letter to your commanding officer and he will straighten it out for you."

The morning we left for the Air Force, Roy and I boarded a bus at the Kansas City, Kansas, Federal Building for Fort Leavenworth in Leavenworth, Kansas, to be sworn in. I believe this was the last time we were actually together. We were assigned to different barracks. We saw each other occasionally at mess hall during the several days we were at Leavenworth. Both of us were sent to Midland, Texas, for basic training, but we were assigned to different squadrons.

I'll never forget the first morning of basic training. A tall, slender, native Texan who spoke with a definite Texan drawl was our drill sergeant. His first words were, "Aren't you lucky to be in this great state of Texas?" The response was more like a groan than an answer. So in a disappointed tone he said, "You're in the Army now. You can gripe all you want, but it won't do you any good." He was a drill sergeant who would never win a popularity contest with his men. Each morning, as the sun was rising, while we were doing our calisthenics, he shouted, "Aren't you lucky to see this beautiful Texas sunrise?" After we made known our thoughts, he said in a sarcastic tone, "Well, why in the hell don't you go home?" At this point, I think a lot of us would have loved to have done so.

When basic training was about completed, we were given options for the type of school we would like to attend. I noticed that mechanic's school was not one of the options. I asked and was granted permission to see the commanding officer. I took the letter the recruiting officer had given me and gave it to him to read. He read it, looked at me, and said, "I'll tell you son, I'd suggest that you put this letter back in your billfold. Report back to your unit, and when we want it, we will ask for it." As I walked back to my barracks, I remembered what the drill sergeant told us that first day, "You're in the Army now. You can gripe all you want, but it won't do you any good." Roy and I never saw each other again until the War was over and we both were civilians.

As basic training was coming to an end, it was almost Christmastime. I wondered how my first Christmas away from home would be. My buddies and I were happy to see how the camp went all out to make our Christmas an enjoyable one. As I was going through some of my Army papers, I found the menu of our Christmas dinner. Even by today's standards, it was a great feast.

I made some very good friends at Midland, Texas. These friends included: Dan Ives from Council Bluffs, Iowa; Irel Green from Kincaid, Kansas; Vernon Wells from Caney, Kansas; and Julian Condron from South Park, Kansas, a suburb of my hometown of Kansas City, Missouri. These friends all decided to sign up for armament school at Buckley Field in Aurora, Colorado, a suburb of Denver. I decided this would be my best choice, too. So Buckley Field was my next destination.

My brother, Captain Harold
W. Henke, enlisted in the
Signal Corp.

Bonnie and Mom standing by the window displaying the
emblem with two stars denoting two family members
were serving our country.

My cousin, Roy Bates (above) and I had planned
to serve our country together, but the Army had
other plans for us.

This was our basic training group in Midland, Texas.

ARMY AIR FORCES BOMBARDIER SCHOOL

MIDLAND, TEXAS

The Army Air Forces Bombardier Christmas dinner brightened my first Christmas away from home.

HEADQUARTERS
ARMY AIR FORCES BOMBARDIER SCHOOL
Office of the Commanding Officer

Midland, Texas

25ᵀᴴ Dec. '42

To the Command:

The turmoil of the past year, occasioned by a fiendish foe, brought many changes in our accustomed living and to our Air Forces a tremendous task of expansion and training. At this School you have maintained that fine tradition and devotion to duty that will bring Victory to our Nation.

It is with a feeling of sincere affection that I wish each of you a very Merry Christmas.

Isaiah Davies
Brig. Gen., U.S. Army

This note from General Davies was included in the Christmas dinner program.

ADVENTURES UNDER FIRE!

CHRISTMAS DINNER
1 9 4 2

Lettuce and Tomato Salad
Iced Celery

Roast Young Turkey   Virginia Baked Ham
Giblet Gravey   Raisin Sauce

Snowflake Potatoes   Buttered Cauliflower
Candied Yams   Cream Corn   Cranberry Sauce   Buttered Peas

Butter
Rolls   Bread

Apple Pie   Fruit Cake   Candy Bar   Mixed Nuts
Ice Cream   Hard Mixed Candy

Coffee   Milk
Lemonade

Cigars   Cigarettes

Assorted Fresh Fruit

The 1942 Christmas dinner menu at Midland, Texas, was one of my best memories of basic training.

Buddies in basic training (left to right) Roy Bates, Al Henke, and Durham.

IMMUNIZATION REGISTER[1]

LAST NAME	FIRST NAME	ARMY SERIAL NO.
Henke,	*Albert C.*	

GRADE	COMPANY	REGT. OR STAFF CORPS	AGE	RACE
			22	

SMALLPOX VACCINE

DATE	TYPE OF REACTION[8]	MED. OFFICER[3]
11-8-42	*drac*	*B. H. PAYNE*
12 43		

TRIPLE TYPHOID VACCINE

SERIES	DATES OF ADMINISTRATION			MED. OFFICER[3]
	1ST DOSE	2D DOSE	3D DOSE	
1st	*11-28-42 comp*	*11-25-42 comp*		*B. H. PAYNE*
2d	*10/11/43 st.*	*FEB 13 1944*		*Ren*
3d				

TETANUS TOXOID

	INITIAL VACCINATION		STIMULATING DOSES		
	DATE	MED. OFF.[3]		DATE	MED. OFF.[3]
1st dose	*11-28-42 comp*			*JUN 4 '43*	*B. H. PAY*
2d dose		*B. H. PAYNE*			
3d dose	*1 - 4 44*				*R.R.*

YELLOW FEVER VACCINE

DATE	LOT NO.	AMOUNT	MED. OFF.[3]
5-12-43	*124*	*½cc*	*B. H. PAYNE*

OTHER VACCINES

DISEASE	DATE	TYPE OF VACCINE	DOSES	MED. OFF.[3]
Cholera	*5-12-43*	MAY 26 '43		*B. H. PAYNE*
Typhus	*5-12-43*	MAY 26 JUN 4 '43		*B. H. PAYNE*
" st 10/11/43				*R.R.*

M. Regan, Capt. , M. C.,
U. S. Army.

16—20202

Chapter

Armament and Gunnery Schools

When my friends and I signed up for technical training, we were not sure we would make it. Over 3,000 men applied, and they only needed 900. We were given a test to determine if we were eligible for the school. The test was difficult and consisted of a lot of math. I felt lucky that I passed and was accepted for the class.

The shipping orders finally came. We were to report to Buckley Field in Aurora, Colorado, for armament school. Our classes started on January 18, 1943. There was a rumor at Midland that we would get a furlough before we started armament school, but there was no time. I was happy that I was accepted for the class and was anxious to get started.

Armament school was scheduled to last 15 weeks, but because they were in a hurry to get the men trained, the class was condensed to nine weeks. The class covered the same material, but it was crammed into nine weeks instead of 15. This made the class very difficult, and it was always a worry that you would get washed out.

On the first day of class, the instructor pointed to the guns we would be studying and said, "Please note this is a caliber .50 machine gun. Never let me hear you refer to it as a 50-caliber machine gun. A 50-caliber machine gun is a cannon on a battleship." This lesson stuck with me. To this day, when I read books about World War II, the guns are almost always referred to as 50-caliber machine guns. I still have the technical manual from the class stating, "This is a caliber .50 machine gun."

I was happy that my four good buddies from Midland, Irel Green, Julian Condron, Vernon Wells, and Dan Ives, were all part of a seven-man class who took this training together. We became even better friends, exchanged home addresses, and decided if we were separated, we would contact each other after the War. (We did get together after the War, with the exception of Julian Condron who was killed in action when his plane went down over Germany.)

The courses in armament school taught us everything we needed to know about guns. We learned the names and functions of all parts of the guns, how to take them apart, clean them, and put them back together. We studied explosives and ammunition. We had classes in synchronization and electricity. The last part of the class was spent on the gunnery range shooting skeet. I really enjoyed this part of the training and was happy that my scores were pretty good.

After a week or so of armament school, we were told that we could sign up for aerial gunnery school. My friends and I all signed up. Again, in order to be eligible for the class, we had to pass several tests and strict physicals. I passed 100 percent, but my friend, Green, was not so lucky. Green wore glasses, and we had to have 20/20 vision to be accepted. This was a big disappointment to all of us. Green was 10 years older than I was and the only married one of our group. His wife, Pearl, constantly sent him boxes of home-made candy and cookies, which Green shared with us. We all thought Pearl was pretty special. Green was an excellent sharpshooter. Before Green entered the service, he did a lot of bird hunting. He was a rural mail carrier; and because of this, he knew most of the farmers in the area who allowed him to hunt on their land. I don't know if I ever topped his record on the gunnery range, but I certainly tried. (Our competition continued after the War. We never missed hunting together on opening day of the quail-hunting season for 35 years. We continued hunting until Green's health failed, and he was no longer able to hunt. Green died several years ago, and not one opening day of quail-hunting season comes along that I don't remember him!) Green ended up as an armorer and was sent to a base in New Jersey. He spent the rest of his service time in the States.

We completed armament school, graduated, and received our diplomas. After graduation, we were promoted to the rank of sergeant and received a raise in pay. We really felt a sense of accomplishment.

Condron, Wells, Ives, and I were anxiously awaiting our orders for aerial gunnery school. They finally came, and on March 20, 1943, we received shipping orders to go to Nellis Air Force Base in Las Vegas, Nevada. We arrived on March 24, and classes started on March 25. This was a five-week class.

One evening, after chow, we were told to meet in back of the barracks for a formation to march to a first aid class. We were told not to go to the nearby PX about 50 feet away. However, Wells decided we should have some ice cream and went to the PX anyway. He bought two quart containers of ice cream, one for me and one for himself. The drill sergeant called us to attention and inspected the ranks. Have you ever stood in formation trying to hide a quart of ice cream? This was the one and only demerit I received during my years in the service. Wells and I were assigned to latrine duty early the next morning. (To this day, we still enjoy ice cream!)

Our first test for a class was a pressure chamber test. After eating a special breakfast and lunch (a bland diet), about 20 of us climbed into a pressure chamber. The air pressure was reduced in the chamber until the air simulated flying at 38,000 feet. The first 18,000 feet was without oxygen masks. If you took the oxygen masks off at 38,000 feet, you could live only about three minutes. We were in the chamber for about four hours. The guy next to me had a hard time. First, his legs went numb. Next, he got cramps and started fighting with the instructor. Then he passed out. At that point, they carried him out. Out of 20 of us, they carried out seven men. If there was the slightest defect, it showed up under this pressure. The only problem I had was a slight pain in my shoulder, which was probably caused by an old high school football injury. I didn't feel it was necessary to report this.

Next, we were trained on how to use and operate a power turret. The turret whirled you around and up and down by simply pushing a button. This was a fun class. Some of our training consisted of firing a 12-gauge shotgun at clay targets from a platform on a truck that was traveling about 30 miles per hour. We were required to hit 30 out of 125 targets. My score was 68. Our next classes were spent shooting machine guns on the ground at targets. The last seven days of the class were in Indian Springs, Nevada, for our air-to-air gunnery training. We flew six of our training missions in an AT-6 and one mission in a B-18 Hudson Bomber. On each mission, we shot 200 rounds of caliber .30 ammunition at a target pulled through the air by another plane. The tips of each person's bullets were dipped in a different color of paint, and we were graded on the number of bullets that hit the target. When we finished shooting, the pilot told us to hang on and he headed back to the base.

Several years ago, I read with interest a book written by Chuck Yeager, in which he stated that he was stationed at Tonapa, California, during this same period of time. He said his job was to fly gunnery students or to pull the targets for them. He stated that he received this assignment as a punishment because he had messed up. I believe that the majority of pilots we flew with on these training missions were sent there for the same reason. After we fired our ammunition and headed back to base, we participated in some of the most exciting flights that I experienced during the War. We hedgehopped, dived, flew up-side-down–you name it! I think they were trying to get us ready for what was yet to come. Chuck Yeager later became a top-notch P-51 pilot and accomplished numerous achievements during his career in the Air Force. He ended up as Brigadier General Yeager.

On May 3, 1943, I graduated from gunnery school, received my gunnery wings, and a staff sergeant rating. That same evening, we received our shipping orders. We were to ship out the next day to Atlantic City, New Jersey.

Our class of 81 gunners from Las Vegas, Nevada, boarded a train to Atlantic City, New Jersey. We were sure we were to get our furlough after we were settled in at Atlantic City, and from there report to an air base for our advanced training. On the way to Atlantic City, we passed through Dan Ives' hometown of Council Bluffs, Iowa. The train didn't even slow down. I thought Ives was going to jump off of the train.

Our housing at Atlantic City was in the Atlantic Towers, a beautiful hotel right on the Boardwalk. Ives and I had a room on the sixth floor overlooking the Atlantic Ocean. This was a pretty fancy place for a bunch of G.I.'s.

We were in Atlantic City for a month, and Wells, Ives, Condron, and I were certain we would get a furlough. We even went so far as to check on train schedules and fares. However, the furlough didn't happen. Wells and Condron shipped out to New York and were issued their overseas address. They ended up in England.

Ives and I thought we were probably going to be sent to a base here, in the United States, and then be assigned to a crew before going overseas. This waiting period was so nerve-racking. We finally received our shipping orders on June 13, 1943. Our orders were to go to Camp Patrick Henry, in Newport News, Virginia. We were not allowed to call home or to write home to tell where we were. From this day on, all mail was censored. After about 10 days at Camp Patrick Henry, our overseas orders came. We were to be transported over on a ship. (Wouldn't you think if you were in the Air Force, you would fly overseas?) The anxiously awaited furlough for which we had hoped was history. When we asked about what happened to the advanced training we were to receive, we were told they didn't know. We would probably receive that when we arrived overseas. As it turned out, our training was on-the-job training. I'll admit, you learn in a hurry under those circumstances.

GUNNER'S INFORMATION FILE

FLEXIBLE GUNNERY

AIR FORCES MANUAL
NO. 20

RESTRICTED

Gunner's Air Force Manual.

THIS IS YOUR GUN

THE CALIBER .50
BROWNING
MACHINE GUN M2
AIRCRAFT, BASIC

With brief instructions on the caliber .30 machine gun and caliber .45 automatic pistol.

RESTRICTED

Caliber .50 machine gun.

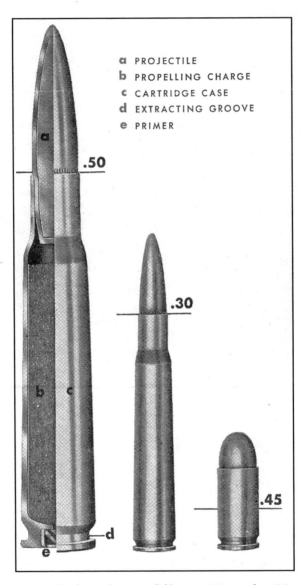

a PROJECTILE
b PROPELLING CHARGE
c CARTRIDGE CASE
d EXTRACTING GROOVE
e PRIMER

Ammunition for caliber .50 and .30 machine guns and .45 pistols.

Julian Condron from
South Park, Kansas.

Irel Green from
Kincaid, Kansas.

Dan Ives from Council
Bluffs, Iowa.

Vernon Wells from
Caney, Kansas.

United States Army

Air Forces Technical School

Be it known that

Private First Class ALBERT C. HENKE

has satisfactorily completed the prescribed

FIGHTER AIRCRAFT ARMORER

course of instruction at the Air Forces Technical School.

In testimony whereof and by virtue of vested authority I do confer upon him this

——DIPLOMA——

Given on this   twentieth   day of March
in the year of our Lord one thousand nine hundred and forty-three

Entered on S/R

R. P. TODD, Lt. Col., AC,
DIRECTOR OF TRAINING

Diploma from Air Forces Technical School in Aurora, Colorado.

P.F.C. Joe Lent (Peoria, Ill. P.F.C. Keith Bell Denver Colo 1324 Broadway
318 Antoinette St. P.F.C. George Ashmore - Denver

P.F.C. Fred G. Green
Kincaid Kansas.

P.F.C. John C. Kessler
Colchester, Illinois

Pfc. Vernon L. Wells
Caney, Kans.

Pfc. Herbert D. Bradnick "Brad"
510 N. Gordon Wichita, Kansas

P.F.C. Charles W. Fuller.
1444 Bluff row
Wichita Kansas.

P.F.C. Howard C. Thompson Detroit, Mich.

Pvt. Dewey W. Walker
N. Dallas St.
Van Alstyne, Texas

P.F.C. Stanley (S+ot 7) Bowman Minneiska Minnesota Rt.
P.F.C. Leo P. Fuller West Des Moines, Iowa
P.F.C. Richard B. Nype 1075 Lexington Road Burlington Wash. Mich.
P.F.C. Fred C. Mack, Jr.
Louisville, Ky. 1509 Manslick Av.
P.F.C. Portis Christianson - Goodridge Minnesota
Pvt. P.F.C Al Blade St. Paul, Minnesota
P.F.C. James Young Alpena Mich.
P.F.C Albert Kevern Jackson, Mich.
Sgt. Harry B. Spence Indianapolis, Ind. 2439 Meridian St.
P.F.C. Al Markowski 1016 Lincoln Ave. Utica, N.Y.
P.F.C. Francis N. De Grand 620 Ro. 18th Street, Escanaba, Michigan
P.F.C Daniel V. Ives Council Bluffs, Iowa
P.F.C Quill Maas, 319 S. Vassar, Wichita, Kansas
P.F.C. Bert Mondor Stillwater, Minn.
P.F.C. Clyde R. Threw 1105 Third ave Peoria, Ill.
P.F.C. Joe Hall Stillwater, Minn.
P.F.C. Dale E. Stroud P.F.C Dick Durand Lewellen Nebr.
Wheeler, Ill.
P.F.C William L. Woodson
2311 Woodson Rd
Overland Mo

Names and addresses of buddies from Buckley Field Air Forces Technical School.

ADVENTURES UNDER FIRE!

This group picture is of my gunnery school class.
Only two men in this group picture survived. Only
11 out of 80 men in our original group managed to
pull through. I consider myself very lucky!

My buddy from gunnery
school, Julian Condron,
was killed over Germany,
in December, 1943.

Chapter

Trip Overseas and Across North Africa

Our orders finally arrived! We were to board the U.S.S. Mariposa on June 24, 1943. The ship was filled to capacity with servicemen and their gear. There were approximately 100 Air Force personnel and hundreds of men from the 45th Infantry Division. Each man was assigned work details for the trip. I was in charge of 17 men, who were responsible for swabbing D-deck every morning. I was a staff sergeant in the Air Force, and the men assigned to me were privates in the infantry. I expected this could have been a problem due to the fact that I was not an infantry-man and had absolutely no experience of being in charge of anyone but myself. However, as long as I worked right with the men, the job was completed without a hitch.

The U.S.S. Mariposa, a luxury liner, was one of many ships the U.S. Government took over during the War to transport troops over-seas. I was billeted in a state room that accommodated six men. The first night, on my bunk, was a welcome letter from President Franklin D. Roosevelt.

I was really tired that first night out, so I hit the sack early. There was a poker game going on in our room, and I didn't know most of the play-ers. I guess those guys gambled most of the night. When I went to bed, I hung my trousers at the end of my bunk and, without a thought, I left my wallet in my pocket. I slept soundly, even with all of the noise. The next morning, as I put on my pants, I realized my wallet was missing.

I spoke to the Navy personnel, but he said, and I agreed, there would not be a chance of recovering my wallet. He said most likely, whoever took the wallet emptied the contents and threw the wallet overboard. We had just received our pay before we left Camp Patrick Henry in Virginia. (In fact, I had several months back pay in my pocket. In the Army, our pay sometimes did not catch up with us for a month or two if we were on the move.) Have you ever traveled overseas without a cent in your pocket? It was at this time, I found out what good friends my Army buddies really were. They lent me money until I was able to get my next pay.

We had nice weather, and it was a great experience sailing on this luxury ship. We pulled into Casablanca Harbor in North Africa seven days after leaving the United States. We landed there on my 23rd birthday, July 1, 1943. As our ship sailed past many warehouses in the port, I was amazed at how many American companies were represented, such as Shell Oil, John Deere, and other companies.

We were billeted in tents on a French airdrome at Casablanca, Morocco, near the beach. The food here was very good. We all had chores, mostly busywork, to keep us physically fit.

We were given passes to go into town to see the city. At the time we were in Casablanca, the heads of states of America, England, and France had a summit meeting. We were sitting on the curb in town when some of them passed by. One that really stood out in my mind was seeing Charles DeGaul of France. Actually, it was not the man, himself, that caught my attention—it was the car in which he was riding. The car was a 1940 maroon-colored Pontiac sedan, exactly like the one I had left parked in the driveway at home when I enlisted. Seeing that car really made me homesick.

We were at Casablanca for about a month when our next orders came. We were to board a 40 & 8 boxcar for a trip of 1,200 miles to Tunis, Tunisia. (The term, 40 & 8 boxcar, means the car could hold 40 men and 8 mules.) We had about 27 men, each with "A" and "B" duffel bags and a flight bag. (An "A" bag contained essentials such as our shaving kits, a "B" bag contained our extra or dirty clothes.) In addition to that, we had K-rations and canned goods. We shared a small gas stove.

The cattle car in which we were riding was not completely enclosed. It had slats on the sides, so we were able to see out. However, the locomotive was a steam engine fired by coal, so the smoke and soot rolled right back on top of us. As if that wasn't bad enough, the countryside was nothing but desert—so we had sand as well as smoke and soot. To top this off, sometime that morning, near Oran, Morocco, the train hit a cow on the tracks. The carcass of the cow became wedged under our car, so blood and pieces of the animal splattered into our car. When the train stopped, several of us tried to pull the cow free, but we were unsuccessful. As time went on and the temperature soared, the odor was almost unbearable.

The gas stove that we were issued malfunctioned and was not usable. This meant that none of the food we had that required heating could be used. We couldn't even make a cup of hot coffee! We opened five-gallon cans of vegetables, which we ate right from the cans. I think my least favorite was a can of beets.

This was such a desolate area. A blacktop road ran parallel to the tracks, but we traveled for miles and saw nothing but desert. However, now and then, we would run into an oasis with a little village where they had water, vineyards, and some date, fig, and nut trees. The train would stop to fill tanks with water for the steam engines. When this happened, we would all get off the train to relieve ourselves, take a quick shower with the hoses, and gather dates, almonds, and grapes from the fields to snack on. When the engineer was ready to leave, he would blow the whistle a couple of times and waited about five minutes for us to board the train.

The first night on the train, Dan Ives, four other guys, and I decided there was no way we could sleep in the cattle car as crowded as it was, so we had the bright idea to spread our blankets on the roof of the train to sleep. At first, this seemed like a good idea. My blanket was at the edge of the roof. During the night, I reached out and could not feel the edge of the car. I sat up and tried to move the guys over as I was close to falling between the cars. All of a sudden, Ives pulled me down. Apparently, during the night, the engineers switched from the steam engine to an electric locomotive. We were now entering the Atlas Mountains. We were just approaching a tunnel, and the electric wires were just inches above our heads. Had Ives not pulled me down, I would have been electrocuted.

The next day, the train picked up a flatcar full of pipe, which was in the car just in front of ours. We got another bright idea that maybe this would be a good place to spend the night and spread out blankets on top of the pipes. This seemed to work out pretty well until the next morning when we found that several Arabs had joined our "bedroom," practically on top of us. We evacuated that area in a hurry.

As we were approaching Bizerte, Tunisia, our train came to a stop to allow hundreds of soldiers and War vehicles to cross the tracks. Montgomery's army had defeated Romell's army, and they were marching the German prisoners to a P.O.W. camp in Bizerte. We figured the Germans would be taking the same train we were on back to the coast for shipment to the U.S. prison camps. When these armies were finished crossing the tracks, the tracks had to be repaired before we could continue our journey. We sat there for a solid day.

We traveled east across Northern Algiers. On the western edge of Algeria, a large ammunition train had exploded the week before, and we could see all the damage to the west side of the city. We could also see the Casbah (a walled city, several stories high) in Algeria at a distance. We continued on east to our destination, Tunis, Tunisia. I've never had a trip like this one, and I hope never to have one like it again.

When we finally reached Tunis, no one was there to meet us; so we were left by the side of the tracks. After our eight-day trip, we were ordered off the train. We spread our blankets on the ground and went to sleep. The next night, we later heard, the Germans bombed this same area. They missed us by one night.

The next morning, some trucks from our new base at Oudina, Tunisia, came and picked us up. The 99th Bomb Group had just moved to Oudina on August 5, and things were still a bit unorganized. The facilities at the camp were all canvas tents. When we checked at Tech Supply to get our tents, we were told that we would have to wait a few days until they could get a tent for us. So, we spent another few nights sleeping on the ground under the stars. We also received our electric flight suits, parachutes, and oxygen masks. The flight suits were suits handed down from the guys who had completed their missions. They told us new suits were not available, but as soon as they got some in, ours would be replaced. When they issued us our parachutes, we were told jokingly, "These parachutes must be really good, because we have not yet had a person bring one back that malfunctioned."

North Africa, being a desert area, was loaded with bugs, lizards, snakes, etc. The thousands of silverfish are one thing that stands out most in my memory. The first week Ives and I were there, our bodies were covered with bumps. We went to the medic, and he told us, "Oh, those are silverfish bites. In a few days your bodies will become immune to them, and they will clear up."

Shortly after this exciting trip, we began our missions, and that's where the real adventure begins. A diary of my 50 missions follows…

ADVENTURES UNDER FIRE!

The U.S.S. Mariposa is the ship that transported us from
Newport News, Virginia, to Casablanca in North Africa.

JULY 7th 1943

THE WHITE HOUSE
WASHINGTON

TO MEMBERS OF THE UNITED STATES ARMY EXPEDITIONARY
FORCES:

You are a soldier of the United States Army.

You have embarked for distant places where
the war is being fought.

Upon the outcome depends the freedom of your
lives: the freedom of the lives of those you love—
your fellow-citizens—your people.

Never were the enemies of freedom more
tyrannical, more arrogant, more brutal.

Yours is a God-fearing, proud, courageous
people, which, throughout its history, has put its
freedom under God before all other purposes.

We who stay at home have our duties to
perform—duties owed in many parts to you. You will
be supported by the whole force and power of this
Nation. The victory you win will be a victory of all
the people—common to them all.

You bear with you the hope, the confidence,
the gratitude and the prayers of your family, your
fellow-citizens, and your President—

Franklin D Roosevelt

I found this message from President Franklin D. Roosevelt
on my bunk the first night on the ship.

ADVENTURES UNDER FIRE!

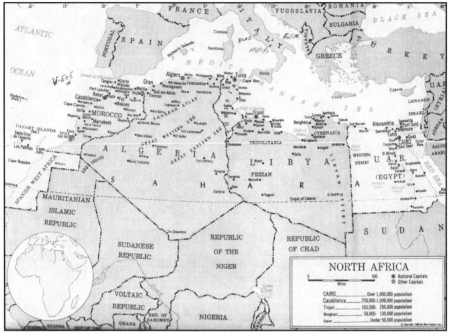

Our trip across North Africa was anything but luxurious!

We saw the sights of North Africa from a 40 & 8 boxcar.

Chapter

My 50-Mission Diary

After Dan Ives and I were assigned our tents, we headed for the orderly room to get our names on a loading list for our first mission. It was not that we were excited about starting our missions, but we knew that the sooner our 50 missions were completed, the sooner we could get back to the good ole U.S.A.

When we went to the orderly room, we learned there was an opening the next morning for two gunners, the tail-position and the ball turret position. Ives took the ball turret, and I took the tail-position. The name of the plane was "Widow-Maker." What a name for a plane with two inexperienced gunners!

Typically, they would wake us for missions any time between 2 a.m. and 6 a.m., depending on the mission destination. While we were being briefed about the mission, ground crews would load the plane with ammunition and supplies.

Shortly after I returned from my missions, I kept a written account of the events that occurred on each mission in a diary, which I hid in the hollowed-out bottom of my shaving kit. I have included in this book copies of the original diary along with a printed copy. On some of the missions, I have included a few comments about what I remember about the mission. Although it has been about 64 years since I flew these missions, the facts stand out as vividly in my mind today as though they took place yesterday. Some experiences are etched into a person's memory…

Author/Editorial Note:

In order to maintain the authenticity of the document, diary entries have been transcribed as they were written in the diary within hours of completing each mission. Some spelling/grammatical errors have been unaltered as they were entered into the actual diary. At the time I wrote this diary, spelling and grammar were the least of my concerns. My primary goal was to record accurate, historical facts regarding each mission.

MISSION #1

DATE: SEPTEMBER 16, 1943
TARGET: BRIDGE & MARSHALLING YARD
LOCATED: BENEVENTO, ITALY
SHIP: WIDOW-MAKER
NUMBER: 244
PILOT: LT. WILSON
HOURS: 6:00
POSITION: TAIL GUNS

No fighters, quite a bit of flak. Target well covered. Bombed at 13,500 feet. Flew Tail-End-Charlie of the group.

Benevento is located about 50 miles northeast of Naples. It's sure a long trip across the Mediterranean with the chance of enemy fighters on Sicily. Our base is located 13 miles south of Tunis in North Africa.

We were the last ship over the target. As I flew tail, I was the last man. Now, I know what they mean by flying "Tail-End-Charlie." A rough spot for your first mission.

Side text: My 50-Mission Diary

1st. MISSION

DATE - SEPT. 16TH 1943
TARGET - BRIDGE AND M/Y
LOCATED - BENEVENTO, ITALY
SHIP - WIDOW-MAKER
NO - 244
PILOT - LT. WILSON
HRS - 6:00
POSITION - TAIL GUNS

No fighters, quite abit
of flak. Target well covered
Bombed at 13.500 feet. I flew
tail-end-charlie of the group.
Benevento is located about
50 miles north-east of Naples. It's
~~sure~~ a long trip across the
Mediterranean with the chance
of enemy fighters on Sicily
Our base is located 13

> *miles south of Tunis in North Africa.*
>
> *We were the last ship over the target. As I flew tail I was the last man, now I know what they mean being "Tail End Charley".*
>
> *A rough spot for your first mission.*

Comments: Mission #1

The morning of September 16, 1943, a jeep came driving through the camp. From a loud speaker we heard, "H-Hour, H-Hour." I thought, "Well here I go, I hope I make it back from my first mission."

We went to headquarters for briefing and then to breakfast before boarding our plane. For Ives and me, this was to be our first time in a B-17. The only flying experience we had was from the back of an AT-6 trainer. On each mission, we wore a flannel flying suit covered by an electric flying suit that plugged into an outlet like a toaster, flannel-lined electric boots, and heated gloves. The planes were not pressurized, and our clothing was the only protection we had from the freezing temperatures. At the altitude we flew, it was not unusual for the temperature to reach 65° below zero.

After flying in the AT-6 trainer, the B-17 seemed large to me. However, the tail section, when loaded with ammunition, was pretty cramped for space. The seat was not a soft, plush bucket seat like you would expect today. It was much like a bicycle seat. This could get very uncomfortable on a long mission of 10 or 11 hours.

On this first mission, our plane was the last plane in the squadron, and ours was the last squadron in formation. This meant that there were approximately 144 planes ahead of us. This was one of the most dangerous positions to be in because, as a rule, the enemy fighters would make a pass at the lead planes and would then work on the last planes in the group that were the most vulnerable to attack. Our plane sat on the runway quite awhile waiting for the other planes to take off and get into formation. At last, it was our turn. I was excited and tense at the same time wondering what would happen next. I expect if we had had the advanced training we were supposed to have received, my questions about what would happen next would have been answered. Perhaps it was just as well. Sometimes the less you know, the less you have to fear...

After we were airborne, the captain got on the intercom and told us to test-fire our guns. I took hold of the guns and they would not move. I thought to myself, "Now what?!" After a few tense moments, I found the latch behind the amour plate to release the guns. We were climbing at a pretty good rate when the captain again announced, "It's time to go on oxygen." I looked around and found a red knob. I turned the dial wide open and had a steady gale of air hitting me in the face all of the way to the target and back. We were lucky it was not a long mission and we didn't encounter a lot of fighters. When we arrived back at the base I overheard Lieutenant Wilson tell the crew-chief, Pete Bezak, to be sure to check the right bank of oxygen tanks because there was a terrific leak somewhere. I never told them that the leak was probably my fault. Well, with the first mission behind me, there were only 49 more to go.

My 50-Mission Diary

MY 50-Mission Diary

Al Henke in Tunis, Tunisia, North
Africa, standing in front of a B-17
Flying Fortress.

MISSION #2

DATE: SEPTEMBER 18, 1943
TARGET: AIR DROME
LOCATED: VITERBO, ITALY
SHIP: BAD PENNY
NUMBER: 509
PILOT: LT. BIOGGIO
HOURS: 6:10
POSITION: WAIST GUNS

A lot of accurate flak, no fighters. Covered target, but enemy planes had moved.

Viterbo is 50 miles north of Rome.

My 50-Mission Diary

2 ND MISSION

DATE- SEPT. 18 TH 1943

TARGET- AIR DROME

LOCATED- VITERBO, ITALY

SHIP - BAD PENNY

NO - 509

PILOT- LT. BIOGGIO

HRS. - 6:10

POSITION- WAIST GUNS

A lot of accurate flak,
no fighters.
Covered target. but
enemy planes had
been moved.
Viterbo is 50 miles
north of Rome.

MISSION #3

DATE: OCTOBER 4, 1943
TARGET: MARSHALLING YARDS
LOCATED: PISA, ITALY
SHIP: SWEATER GIRL
NUMBER: 472
PILOT: LT. TRENTADUE
HOURS: 6:00
POSITION: WAIST GUNS

Still no fighters, heavy flak. Hit target.

Passed near Sardinia and Corsica on our way up also coming back. Pisa is on the western coast of Italy, on the Ligurian Sea. We could spot the Leaning Tower of Pisa from the air.

3RD MISSION

DATE - Oct. 4 Th 1943
TARGET - MARSHALLING YARDS
LOCATED - PISA, ITALY
SHIP - SWEATER GIRL
NO. - 472
PILOT - LT. TRENTADUE
HRS. - 6:00
POSITION - WAIST GUNS

Still no fighters, heavy flak. Hit target.
Passed near Sardinia and Corsica on our way up also coming back
Pisa is on the western coast of Italy on the Ligurian sea. We could spot the leaning tower of Pisa from the air.

My 50-Mission Diary

MISSION #4

DATE: OCTOBER 5, 1943
TARGET: MARSHALLING YARDS
LOCATED: BOLOGNA, ITALY
SHIP: MISS PEGGY
NUMBER: 883
PILOT: CAPT. BUCK
HOURS: 7:20
POSITION: BALL TURRET

No fighters, heavy flak, leveled the target. Flew ball turret for the first time today. Quite an experience. You certainly get a view of the target from this position. Bologna is located in North Central Italy, a large railroad junction.

4Th MISSION
DATE - Oct. 5Th 1943
TARGET - MARSHALLING YARDS
LOCATED - BOLOGNA, ITALY
SHIP - MISS PEGGY
NO. - 883
PILOT - CAPT. BUCK
HRS. - 7.20
POSITION - BALL TURRET

No fighters, heavy
flak, leveled the target.
I flew ball turret for
the first time to-day.
Quite an experience. You
certainly get a view of
the target from this
position. Bologna is
located in North Central
Italy, a large railroad
junction.

MISSION #5

DATE: OCTOBER 9, 1943
TARGET: AIR FIELD
LOCATED: SALONIKA, GREECE
SHIP: LEAD SHIP OF SQUADRON
NUMBER: 471
PILOT: CAPT. BUCK
HOURS: 8:20
POSITION: BALL TURRET

No fighters but flak was very heavy and accurate. We went over target twice and picked up eight holes in our ship. My heat suit shorted out and caught on fire. Finally pulled the plug and pinched out the fire. Have a burned spot about the size of a half-dollar on the inside of my right thigh. Guess that's the first scar.

I just about froze to death coming back. Had to stay in the ball turret without heat for three hours due to the fact we were in enemy territory all the way across Southern Italy and Sicily.

Salonika is located in Northeast Greece just south of Bulgaria. Flew part way over the Aegean Sea. Could see Malta on our return trip.

> 5TH MISSION
> DATE - Oct. 9Th 1943
> TARGET - AIR FIELD
> LOCATED - SALONIKA, GREECE
> SHIP - LEAD SHIP OF SQUADRON
> NO. - 471
> PILOT - CAPT. BUCK
> HRS. - 8:20
> POSITION - BALL TURRET
>
> No fighters - but flak
> was very heavy and
> accurate. We went over
> target twice and picked
> up eight holes in our
> ship. My heat suit shorted
> out and caught on fire. Finally
> pulled the plug and pinched
> out the fire. Have a burned
> spot about the size of a half
> dollar on the inside of my

Comments: Mission #5

This was my second mission in the ball turret position. The ball turret position gives you a better view of what is going on, but I much prefer the tail gun position. When my heat suit caught on fire, I thought for sure I had been hit by flak. In such a cramped space, I had a time pinching out the fire in my heat suit. I don't know what kept me from freezing to death without an operating heat suit in 65° below zero conditions. It took 4 ½ hours to return to base. Although I had a burned spot on my thigh, I considered myself lucky.

right thigh. Guess
that's the first scar.
Just about froze to death
coming back. Had to stay
in the ball turret without
heat for 3 hours due to
the fact we were in enemy
territory all the
way across southern
Italy and Sicily.
Salonika is located in
northeast of Greece just
south of Bulgaria. Flew
part way over the Aegean
Sea. Could see Malta
on our return trip.

After we landed, I went back to Tech Supply to see if they had a replacement heat suit. Again, I was told that they still hadn't received their new supply, but gave me a roll of electrical tape and said perhaps I could patch it so it would work. From there, I stopped by Doc Beal's tent so he could look at my burn. He gave me a shot of whiskey and a tube of ointment and said, "Put this ointment on it and it should be just fine in a few days,"…and it was!

I'm dressed for "work" in my heat suit, oxygen mask, and parachute. (The heat suit didn't provide much heat after shorting out and burning me.)

My 50-Mission Diary

MISSION #6

DATE: OCTOBER 14, 1943
TARGET: MARSHALLING YARDS
LOCATED: TERNI, ITALY
SHIP: MISS PEGGY
NUMBER: 883
PILOT: CAPT. BUCK
HOURS: 6:00
POSITION: BALL TURRET

Leveled the yards and started several oil fires. About twelve ME-109's and FW-190's attacked as we came off the target. We beat them off and was jumped 30 minutes later out at sea by 25 more. The second bomb group lost a ship just behind us. We knocked down three fighters. I fired 350 rounds. Our first taste of fighters. They look pretty mean coming in at you with those guns blazing.

It feels good to get home this time.

Terni is in Central Italy approximately 50 miles northeast of Rome.

We ran into a few of Gorings crack pilots today. They had their prop hubs painted yellow. That indicates they have at least five kills to their credit.

6 TH MISSION

DATE - OcT. 14 TH 1943
TARGET - MARSHALLING YARDS
LOCATED - TERNI, ITALY
SHIP - MISS PEGGY
NO. - 883
PILOT - CAPT. BUCK
HRS. - 6:00
POSITION - BALL TURRET

Leveled the yards and
started several oil fires.
About twelve ME109s and FW
190 s. attacked as we came
off the target. We beat them
off and was jumped 30 min.
later out at sea by 25 more.
The second B. Gp. lost a
ship just behind us. We
knocked down three fighters.
I fired 350 rounds. First

taste of fighters. They
look pretty mean coming
in at you with those guns
blazing.
It felt good to get home
this time.
Terni is in central
Italy approximately 50
miles north east of Rome.
We ran into a few
of Goaring's crack pilots
to day. They had their
prop hubs painted
yellow, that indicates
they have at least five
kills to their credit.

Comments: Mission #6

This was my first experience with fighters. What a rough day! I had heard of the German fighters with their propeller hubs painted yellow, indicating that they had at least five kills. The fact that we were going at it with some of Hitler's Ace fighters was really scary. This mission was one I will never forget. It was a relief to get back to the base.

The sleeping quarters were not exactly five-star hotel accommodations.

MISSION #7

DATE: OCTOBER 29, 1943
TARGET: MARSHALLING YARDS
LOCATED: GENOA, ITALY
SHIP: LADY LUCK
NUMBER: 507
PILOT: LT. BEAUR
HOURS: 8:15
POSITION: BALL TURRET

Some flak and six fighters. Picked up two flak holes. One 17 behind us exploded in the air, a direct hit by flak.

South coast of North Italy. A large sea port. Saw a lot of ships heading out to sea, guess they figured we were after them.

7ᵗʰ MISSION

DATE - Oct. 29 ᵗʰ 1943
TARGET - MARSHALLING YARDS
LOCATED - GENOA, ITALY
SHIP - LADY LUCK
NO. - 507
PILOT - LT. BEAUR
HRS. - 8:15
POSITION - BALL TURRET

Some flak and six fighters. Picked up two flak holes. One 17 behind us exploded in the air, a direct hit by flak. South coast of north Italy. A large sea port saw a lot of ships heading out to sea, guess they figured we were after them.

Comments: Mission #7

This was the first mission I flew in which another plane in our own squadron took a direct hit and went down in flames. This really shook us up, but we just had to concentrate on the job we were there to do and hope that next burst of flak didn't take us out, too.

MISSION #8

DATE: OCTOBER 30, 1943
TARGET: BALL BEARING FACTORY
LOCATED: TURIN, ITALY
SHIP: LADY LUCK
NUMBNER: 507
PILOT: LT. BEAUR
HOURS: 8:15
POSITION: BALL TURRET

No flak, no fighters. Hit target hard.

Located in Northwest Italy near French border, just south of Switzerland.

8TH MISSION

DATE - Oct. 30TH 1943
TARGET - BALL BEARING FACTORY
LOCATED - TURIN, ITALY
SHIP - LADY LUCK
NO. - 507
PILOT - LT. BEAUR
HRS. - 8:15
POSITION - BALL TURRET

No flak. No fighters.
Hit target hard.
Located north west Italy
near French border just
South of Switzerland.

MISSION #9

DATE: NOVEMBER 2, 1943
TARGET: MESSERSCHMITT FACTORY
LOCATED: WEINER-NEUSTADT, AUSTRIA
SHIP: SMILEY
NUMBER: 244
PILOT: LT. BORMAN
HOURS: 11:20
POSITION: WAIST GUNS

The most exciting raid so far. About 75 Libs joined our four groups of 17's. Sky was black with flak, we were attacked by 75 fighters. I saw four B-24's go down in a sheet of flame. We lost two 17's and seven 24's. Supposed to have knocked down 22 enemy fighters. Landed at Sicily and spent the night under the ship. One tail gunner killed in our group.

My longest mission so far. We knew this one was going to be tough. H-hour was at 3:00 a.m. After briefing we had to go back to our tents to pick up blankets. Only planes equipped with To-kyo tanks were scheduled to fly. That meant deep penetration and overnight stop for refueling. We landed on a fighter strip in Sicily. A tight fit for a fortress to land with wrecked gliders all over the field. I slept on the run-way within 20 feet of the dead tail gunner mentioned above. Didn't get much sleep. Took off for Africa after chow. Hope I don't see any more like this one.

9TH MISSION

DATE - NOV. 2ND 1943

TARGET - MESSERSCHMITT FACTORY

LOCATED - WEINER - NEUSTADT, AUSTRIA

SHIP - SMILEY

NO. - 244

PILOT - LT. BORMAN

HRS. - 11:20

POSITION - WAIST GUNS

The most exciting raid so far. About 75 libs joined our four groups of 17's. Sky was black with flak, we were attacked by 75 fighters. I saw four B24's go down in a sheet of flame. We lost two 17's and seven 24's. Suppose to have knocked down 22 enemy fighters. Landed at Sicily and spent the night under the ship. One tail gunner killed in our group.

My longest mission so
far. We knew this one was
going to be rough. H-Hour
at 3:00 AM. After breifing we
had to go back to our tents
to pick up blankets. Only
planes equipped with Tokyo
tanks were scheduled to fly.
That meant deep pentration
and over night stop for
refueling. We landed on
a fighter strip in Sicily.
A tight fit for a fortress
to land with wrecked gliders
all over the field. I slept
on the run way with in 20 feet
of the dead tail gunner mentioned
above. I didn't get much
sleep. Took off for Africa
after chow. Hope I don't
see any more like this one.

My 50-Mission Diary

Comments: Mission #9

Eleven hours and 20 minutes is a long time. Can you imagine the pressure the pilot must have felt after going through all of the flak, the never-ending enemy fighters, and then landing on a field that was not meant for a bomber to land on? I flew the waist gun position on this mission and could see the pilot and co-pilot as they maneuvered the plane to a safe landing. These guys didn't have an easy go.

In the diary, I mentioned that only planes equipped with Tokyo tanks were scheduled to fly. This is because these planes had extra fuel tanks in their wings and could fly further distances. On flights this long, we did not have the luxury of fighter planes because they did not have fuel tanks large enough to fly that far.

This is another mission I will never forget. The dead tail gunner in the ship next to ours really gave me an eerie feeling. I couldn't help but think that if this had been me lying there, would my mom have been able to handle it? I wondered if she would really get my insurance, etc. I wondered how I would be able to get on a plane for the next mission. By this time, I had the feeling, as did most of the guys I flew with, that we might never complete our missions and return home…

MISSION #10

DATE: NOVEMBER 8, 1943
TARGET: BALL BEARING FACTORY
LOCATED: TURIN, ITALY
SHIP: LADY LUCK
NUMBER: 507
PILOT: CAPT. SHAW
HOURS: 6:15
POSITION: TAIL GUNS

Some flak, six fighters. Nice view of Switzerland. Would have been a good chance to get out of the war, only 30 miles away.

Flew tail for Capt. Shaw today. His home is in Marshall, Missouri. He recently transferred into our squadron. Was a pilot for Elliot Roosevelt.

10TH MISSION
DATE - NOV. 8TH 1943
TARGET- BALL BEARING FACTORY
LOCATED- TURIN, ITALY
SHIP - LADY LUCK
NO. - 507
PILOT- CAPT. SHAW
HRS. - 6:15
POSITION - TAIL GUNS

Some flak, six fighters. Nice view of Switzerland. Would have been a good chance to get out of the war, only 30 miles away. Flew tail for Capt. Shaw today. His home is in Marshall Mo. He recently transferred into our squadron. Was a pilot for Elliot Roosevelt.

Comments: Mission #10

If a plane went down in Switzerland, the men were interned until the end of the War. Switzerland would not send them home, nor would they allow them to go back to their outfit because Switzerland was a neutral country.

I felt like I met a neighbor when I met Captain Shaw. He was from Marshall, Missouri, and I spent my teenage years working on my Uncle's farm in nearby Brunswick, Missouri. (The two towns are about 30 miles apart.)

My 50-Mission Diary

MISSION #11

DATE: NOVEMBER 10,1943
TARGET: MARSHALLING YARDS
LOCATED: BOLZANO, ITALY
SHIP: LEAD SHIP OF GROUP
NUMBER: 471
PILOT: MAJ. MacDONALD
HOURS: 9:00
POSITION: TAIL GUNS

Flew clear across Northern Italy dropping leaflets and destroyed the yards at Bolzano. Attacked by twelve fighters and we knocked down two of them. Saw one fortress out of second bomb group go down in spin. 4 chutes came out. It was 45 degrees below zero.

Our squadron commander returned from the hospital yesterday and formed a new crew. I was lucky to be selected as tail gunner for squadron crew. Maj. MacDonald is a pre-war cadet, only 24 years old and a top notch pilot. We led the group today. I have a new duty now–keeping track of all four of our squadrons. At briefing I received a flight list of all planes in our group showing the pilot's name and plane number and position in formation. Any plane hit or turning back I have to report to the Major. Sure feels good to be part of a regular crew.

Extreme North Italy near the Austrian border.

11Th MISSION

DATE - NOV. 10Th 1943

TARGET - MARSHALLING YARDS

LOCATED - BOLZANO, ITALY

SHIP - LEAD SHIP OF GROUP

NO. - 471

PILOT - MAJ. MACDONALD

HRS. - 9:00

POSITION - TAIL GUNS

Flew clear across northern Italy dropping leaflets and destroyed the yards at Bolzano. Attacked by twelve fighters and we knocked down two of them. Saw one fortress out of second B. G. go down in spin, 4 chutes came out. It was 45 degrees below zero.

Our squadron Commander

returned from hospital
yesterday and formed a new
crew. I was lucky to be
selected as tail gunner for
squadron crew. Maj. MacDonald
is a pre-war cadet only 24
years old and a top notch
pilot. We led the old group
to day. I have a new
duty now - keeping tract
of all 4 of our squadrons,
at briefing I receive a flight
list of all planes in our
group showing the pilots
name and plane number and
position in formation. any
plane hit or turning back
I have to report to the
Major. Sure feels good
to be part of a regular crew.
Extreme north Italy near Austrian
border.

Comments: Mission #11

A squadron consisted of nine planes that flew in formation groups of three, which included the lead ship, right-wing, and left-wing planes. The 416th squadron had nine planes. The 99th Bomb Group consisted of four squadrons, which included 36 planes.

B-17s flew in a typical formation like this.

MISSION #12

DATE: NOVEMBER 24, 1943
TARGET: DOCKS-HARBOR-AMM. DUMPS
LOCATED: TOULON, FRANCE
SHIP: LEAD SHIP ROBERT E. LEE
NUMBER: 482
PILOT: MAJ. MAC
CO-PILOT: GEN. ATKINSON
HOURS: 6:50
POSITION: TAIL GUNS

Some flak and four fighters. Hits on ships, docks, buildings and oil and ammunitions dumps. We received a commendation for the raid. One hundred miles off Corsica, 502 went down. They dropped back out of formation, the crew bailed out and the plane plunged into the sea. There has been no word received as to what happened or if any of the crew was saved. New crew on their 2nd mission.

General Atkinson flew as our co-pilot today. We led the whole 12th Air Force of heavy bombers.

Sorry to see 502 go down. I knew all of the men aboard. Their tent is next to ours. Sure quiet over there tonight.

Southern tip of France on the Gulf of Lions.

12Th MISSION

DATE - NOV. 22^{#a} 1943
TARGET - DOCKS - HARBOR - AMM. DUMPS
LOCATED - TOULON. FRANCE
SHIP - LEAD SHIP OF GROUP
NO. - 482 ROBT. E. LEE
PILOT - MAJ. MAC. - CO-PILOT GEN. ATKINSON
HRS. - 6:50
POSITION - TAIL GUNS

Some flak and four fighters.
Hits on ships, docks, buildings
and oil & ammunition dumps.
We received a accomadation for
the raid. One hundred miles off
Corsica 502 went down. They dropped
back out of formation, the crew
bailed out and the plane plunged
into the sea. There has been
no word received as to what happened,
or if any of the crew were saved.
New crew on their 2nd mission.

General Atkinson flew as
our co-pilot to-day. We
led the whole 12th air force
of Heavy bombers.
Sorry to see 502 go down
I knew all the men aboard.
Their tent is next to ours.
Sure quite over there to-
night.

Southern tip of France
on the Gulf of Lions.

Comments: Mission #12

It was an honor to fly on the same ship as Major Mac
(Major MacDonald) and General Atkinson. But how sad it was
to see #502 go down. Their tent was right next to ours. It was
like losing the whole family of 10 who lived next door. You always think of what a loss it was to their families.

These men are crew members on my squadron at our camp in Foggia, Italy. Front row (left to right): Lieutenant Ervin Haron, Navigator, Technical Sergeant Ross McKinney, Radio Operator/Gunner. Back row (left to right): Captain Burnham Shaw, Co-Pilot, Staff Sergeant Howard Carter, Waist Gunner, Lieutenant Don Hemmingson, Bombardier.

MISSION #13

DATE: NOVEMBER 29, 1943
TARGET: AIR FIELD
LOCATED: FIANO ROMANO, NEAR ROME
SHIP: ROBT. E. LEE (LEAD)
NUMBER: 482
PILOT: MAJ. MAC
HOURS: 6:40
POSITION: TAIL GUNS

No flak, no fighters, target covered by clouds, had to return with our bombs. Weather was bad all of the way.

Second mission on the Robert E. Lee. This will be our ship. Has Studebaker engines, sounds different than the other planes with Wright Cyclones.

I received my draft notice in a letter from my mother yesterday. Had some fun with the Major. As we were getting in the plane to take-off I told him I couldn't go today as this card told me to report without fail to the Selective Service Board at St. John & Belmont, in Kansas City, Missouri. He suggested I let them come and get me.

13Th MISSION

DATE - 29Th NOV. 1943
TARGET - AIR FIELD·FIANO ROMANO
LOCATED - NEAR ROME
SHIP - LEAD SHIP OF GROUP
NO. - 482 ROBT-E. LEE
PILOT - MAJ. MAC.
HRS. - 6:40
POSITION - TAIL GUNS

No flak, no fighters.
target covered by clouds.
had to return with our bombs.
Weather was bad all the
way.
~~First~~ SECOND mission on the ROBT.E LEE
This will be our ship. Has
Studebaker engines, sounds
different than the other planes
with Wright Cyclones
I received my draft notice

in a letter from my
mother yesterday. Had
some fun with the ~~maj~~ major.
As we were getting in the
plane to takeoff I told
him I couldn't go to day
as this card told me to
report with out fail to
the Selective Service
Board at St John & Belmont
in Kansas City, Mo.

He suggest I let them
come and get me.

This B-17 is coming in for a landing at the airstrip.

MISSION #14

DATE: DECEMBER 14, 1943
TARGET: AIR FIELD
LOCATED: NEAR ATHENS, GREECE
SHIP: ROBERT E. LEE (LEAD)
NUMBER: 482
PILOT: MAJ. MAC
HOURS: 5:35
POSITION: TAIL GUNS

Flew directly over the city, ran into a lot of flak and about ten fighters. One ship in 2nd BG went down behind us over the city. Was hit by flak, banked to the left, three chutes came out, ship went into a spin and exploded. We had a P-38 escort. Seen some real dog-fights. First day with fighter escort. Feels good to have them with us. Nice view of the city, only thing we couldn't see much from five miles up.

14 TH MISSION
DATE - DEC. 14 TH 1943
TARGET - AIR FIELD
LOCATED - NEAR ATHENS, GREECE
SHIP - LEAD SHIP OF GROUP
NO. - 482 - ROBT. E. LEE.
PILOT - MAJ. MAC.
HRS. - 5:35
POSITION - TAIL GUNS

Flew directly over the city
run into a lot of flak and about
ten fighters. One ship in 2nd B.C.
went down behind us over the
city. Was hit by flak, banked
to the left, three chutes came
out, ship went into a spin and
exploded. We had a P 38 escort.
seen some real dog-fights.
First day with fighter escort
fells good to have them with
us. nice view of the city

My 50-Mission Diary

only thing we couldn't
see much from five
mile up.

Comments: Mission #14

This was our first mission from Foggia, Italy. The 99th Bomb Group had just moved there the day before. As soon as we landed in Foggia, we had to erect our tents and get settled before our mission early the next morning. The ground crew traveled to Italy by ship and was not available to service the planes. We assisted the crew chief in getting the planes ready and helped to load the bombs. The move to Italy was quite interesting. All of our gear, tents, etc. were loaded into the plane and away we went.

Sometime earlier, the crew had adopted a cat, or I should say, the cat adopted us. It was decided that we would not leave it behind. We thought if we put it in the ball turret and closed the hatch, it would be safe and not wander around and fall out of the plane. When we arrived in Foggia, we opened the hatch and the cat jumped out. We did not see it for a day or two. I guess it didn't like the ball turret any better than I did. It must have gotten air sick. The entire turret was covered with diarrhea and vomit. We thoroughly cleaned the turret, but the odor remained for a long time. I did not envy Wojack who had to fly the turret position, the next day.

Flying out of Italy was quite different than flying out of Africa. It meant that our flights were not quite as long and we were able to have some fighter escorts—a very welcome addition. However, the weather in Italy was completely different from the dry desert climate in North Africa. It was very swampy and muddy. The runways there were constructed of steel matting. At times, when we had a hard rain before we took off, the mud would ooze up between the matting. When the heavy bombers took off, the slip-stream caused a lot of mud to be deposited on the windows of the tail. It was impossible to see out of the windows. I knew that this had to be cleaned off before we reached the higher altitude when it would freeze and my chances of seeing fighters coming at me would be very slim. This problem happened several times in Italy. So when we became airborne, at about 5,000 feet in the air, I tied a cotton mattress cover (which I always carried on flights) around the gun mount and the other end around my waist. I then opened the small window on the left side, the only one that opened, crawled out as far as I could, and wiped the window on the right side, the front, and the left side. At the time I flew these missions, I had a 29-inch waist and could just barely squeeze through that window. I guess God was with me because I didn't get sucked out of the plane. I don't recall asking the other gunners what they did to solve this problem, but in later years, I often wondered how they handled it.

My 50-Mission Diary

Loading a plane on a muddy runway in Italy was no easy task for this crew.

Mud would ooze up from the steel matting on the runway in Foggia, Italy.

MISSION #15

DATE: DECEMBER 19, 1943
TARGET: CITY PROPER
LOCATED: INNSBRUCK, AUSTRIA
SHIP: ROBERT E. LEE (LEAD)
NUMBER: 482
PILOT: MAJ. MAC
HOURS: 6:00
POSITION: TAIL GUNS

Attacked by 75 or 80 fighters, destroyed 37 and 22 probable. Flak heavy, accurate and intense. Saw two 17's go down in flames over the Alps. Five chutes out of one and three out of the other. Saw two 17's go down near the water. All together we lost 7 fortresses and 4 Libs. Our right wingman was shot up bad. Three of the men injured seriously. The bombardier died two days later. Our group lost two ships, six men wounded and three killed. Our ship was shot up some. Our top turret knocked down a fighter.

We came off the target and ended up right over the famous "Berchesgaden," Hitler's hide-a-way. I wonder if he was home? It looked like the enemy fighters were coming right out of the ground. Actually they were coming off an Autobon in the valley. We ran into a hornet's nest today. I like being in the lead ship but the first attack is always on the front, then they work on the rear.

Near the southern border of Germany, not far from Brinner Pass.

15ᵗʰ MISSION

DATE - DEC. 19ᵗʰ 1943

TARGET - CITY PROPER

LOCATED - INNSBRUCK, ~~GERMANY~~ Austria

SHIP - LEAD SHIP OF GROUP

NO. - 482 ROBT. E. LEE

PILOT - MAJ. MAC.

HRS. - 6:00

POSITION - TAIL GUNS

Attacked by 75 or 80 fighters destroyed 37 and 22 probables. Flak heavy, accurate and intense. Saw two 17s go down in flames over the alps, five chutes out of one and three out of the other. Saw two 17's go down over the water. All together we lost 7 forts and 4 libs. Our right wing man was shot up bad, three of the men injured seriously. The bombardier died

Mission #15

two days later. Our group
lost two ships, six men
wounded and thru killed.
Our ship was shot up some.
Our top turret knocked down
a fighter.
We came off the target
and ended up right over
the famous "Berchesgaden",
Hitler's Hide-a-way.
I wonder if he was home?
It looked like the enemy
fighters were coming right
out of the ground. Actually
they were coming off an autobon in the valley, We ran
into a hornets nest to-day.
I like being in the lead
ship but the first attack is
always on the front, then they
work on the rear. Near southern
border of germany, not far from Brenner
Pass.

Comments: Mission #15

The top turret gunner was Howard P. Carter who was credited with knocking down a German fighter. He was a Kansas City resident. He and I attended Northeast High School and were in the same history class. Small world!

The wreckage of a German fighter sat near our campsite.

MISSION #16

DATE: DECEMBER 25, 1943
TARGET: MARSHALLING YARDS
LOCATED: UDINE, ITALY
SHIP: FORT ALAMO II (LEAD)
NUMBER: 696
PILOT: CAPT. SHAW
HOURS: 6:00
POSITION: TAIL GUNS

Very cloudy, could not see target so returned with bombs. 60 below zero.

What a Christmas!

Really found a mess when we landed. Had quite a wind and rain storm. Our tents were down and everything soaked. We ate our turkey dinner in a cold rain sitting on the ground.

Located northeast corner of Italy. Surprised we didn't run into fighters. Could see plenty of fighter strips, but nothing showed up.

16th MISSION

DATE - DEC. 25th 1943 CHRISTMAS DAY

TARGET - MARSHALLING YARDS.

LOCATED - UDINE, ITALY

SHIP - FORT ALAMO II

NO. - 696   LEAD - SQUADRON

PILOT - CAPT. SHAW

HRS. - 6:00

POSITION - TAIL GUNS

Very cloudy, could not
see target so returned with
bombs, -60 below zero.

What a Christmas!

Really found a mess when
we landed. Had quite a wind
and rain storm. Our tents
were down and everything soaked
We eat our turkey dinner in

a cold rain setting on
the ground.
Located north east corner
of Italy. Surprised we
didn't run into fighters.
Could see plenty of fighter
strips, but nothing showed
up.

When I left my tent for a mission, I never knew if I would return.

My 50-Mission Diary

MISSION #17

DATE: DECEMBER 28, 1943
TARGET: MARSHALLING YARDS
LOCATED: RIMINI, ITALY
SHIP: FORT ALAMO II (LEAD)
NUMBER: 696
PILOT: CAPT. SHAW
HOURS: 4:30
POSITION: TAIL GUNS

Dropped our bombs in heart of city. No fighters, no flak. Went over target twice with bad oil leak. Came home on three engines.

Rimini is located on the east coast of Italy about halfway up on the Adriatic Sea.

17 TH MISSION
DATE - DEC. 28 TH 1943
TARGET - MARSHALLING YARDS.
LOCATED - RIMINI, ITALY
SHIP - FORT ALAMO II
NO. - 696   LEAD - SQUADRON
PILOT - CAPT. SHAW
HRS. - 4:30
POSITION - TAIL GUNS.

Dropped our bombs in
heart of city. No fighters, no
flak. Went over target twice
with bad oil leak. Came
home on three engines.
Rimini is located on
the east coast of Italy about
half way up the on the
Adriatic Sea.

MISSION #18

DATE: JANUARY 4, 1944
TARGET: GERMAN HEADQUARTERS, CITY PROPER
LOCATED: SOFIA, BULGARIA
SHIP: SPOOFER   (LEAD WING)
NUMBER: 522
PILOT: MAJ. MAC
HOURS: 6:15
POSITION: TAIL GUNS

Target covered, could not drop bombs. A few bursts of heavy accurate flak and three FW-190's made one pass at our squadron. They hit one ship but did no damage. Our ship lead all four groups. The first mission over Bulgaria by any ship from this theater.

Our mission today took us over Albania and Yugoslavia.

18 Th MISSION

DATE - JAN. 4 Th 1944

TARGET - GERMAN HEAD QUARTERS - CITY PROPE

LOCATED - SOFIA, BULGARIA

SHIP - SPOOFER

NO. - 522 LEAD-WING

PILOT - MAJ. MAC.

HRS. - 6:15

POSITION - TAIL GUNS

Target covered, could not drop
bombs. A few bursts of heavy,
accurate flak and three F.W 190's
made one pass at our squadron.
They hit one ship but did no
damage. Our ship lead all four
groups. The first mission over
Bulgaria by any ship from this
theater.

Our mission to day took us
over Albania and Yugoslavia.

MISSION #19

DATE: JANUARY 7, 1944
TARGET: AIR CRAFT FACTORY
LOCATED: WEINER-NEUSTADT, AUSTRIA
SHIP: SWEATER GIRL LEAD SQUADRON
NUMBER: 472
PILOT: CAPT. SHAW
HOURS: 4:30
POSITION: TAIL GUNS

Turned back eighty miles from target due to bad weather. Flew around over Hungary, Austria and Yugoslavia, trying to find a target open.

Returned with bombs.

19Th MISSION

DATE - JAN. 7 Th 1944

TARGET - AIR CRAFT FACTORY

LOCATED - WEINER - NEUSTADT, AUSTRIA

SHIP - 472   SWEATER GIRL

NO - 472   LEAD - SQUADRON

PILOT - CAPT. SHAW

HRS. - 4:30

POSITION - TAIL GUNS

    Turned back eighty miles from target due to bad weather. Flew around over Hungary - Austria and Yugoslavia, trying to find a target open.
    Returned with bombs.

MISSION #20

DATE: JANUARY 8, 1944
TARGET: AIR CRAFT FACTORY
LOCATED: REGGIO EMILIA, ITALY
SHIP: ROBT. E. LEE (LEAD)
NUMBER: 482
PILOT: CAPT. SHAW
HOURS: 6:00
POSITION: TAIL GUNS

No flak a few fighters. Hit ME-109 factory, marshalling yards and castor oil plant.

Did a good job on target.

North Central Italy.

20th MISSION

DATE - JAN. 8th 1944

TARGET - AIR CRAFT FACTORY

LOCATED - REGGIO EMILIA, ITALY

SHIP - ROBT. E. LEE   LEAD - SQUADR

NO. - 482

PILOT - CAPT. SHAW

HRS. - 6:00

POSITION - TAIL GUNS

No flak a few fighters. Hit ME.109 factory, marshalling yards and castor oil plant. Did a good job on target.

North Central Italy

MISSION #21

DATE: JANUARY 9, 1944
TARGET: DOCKS
LOCATED: POLA, ITALY
SHIP: ROBT. E. LEE
(LEAD - GROUP)
NUMBER: 482
PILOT: MAJ. MAC
HOURS: 4:00
POSITION: TAIL GUNS

No fighters, flak moderate, light and accurate. Target was destroyed. We could see ships on the move in every direction. They were heading for the open sea.

Located near Trieste on the Gulf of Venice.

21ST MISSION
DATE - JAN. 9TH 1944
TARGET - DOCKS
LOCATED - POLA, ITALY
SHIP - ROBT. E. LEE   LEAD-GROUP
NO. - 482
PILOT - MAJ. MAC.
HRS. - 4:00
POSITION - TAIL GUNS

No fighters, flak moderate,
light and accurate.
Target destroyed.
We could see ships on the
move in every direction. They
were heading for the open sea.

Located near Trieste on the
Gulf of Venice.

MISSION #22

DATE: JANUARY 10, 1944
TARGET: GERMAN HEADQUARTERS
LOCATED: SOFIA, BULGARIA
(HEART OF CITY)
SHIP: ROBT. E. LEE (LEAD)
NUMBER: 482
PILOT: CAPT. SHAW
HOURS: 5:00
POSITION: TAIL GUNS

Hit by eighty-five fighters, flak intense, heavy and accurate. Met the fighters just before bombs away and had them for twenty-five minutes. Shot over two hundred rounds, hit a ME-109 but did no damage. Our waist gunner knocked one down at 4:00 o'clock level. Our squadron destroyed four and a probable on one. Target well covered. 347th Sq. lost a ship. Sky was black with flak.

My 50-Mission Diary

My 50-Mission Diary

22ND MISSION

DATE - JAN. 10 Th 1944

TARGET - GERMAN HEADQUARTERS

LOCATED - SOFIA, BULGARIA - HEART OF CITY

SHIP - ROBT. E. LEE   LEAD - SQUADRON

NO. - 482

PILOT - CAPT. SHAW

HRS. - 5:00

POSITION - TAIL GUNS

Hit by eighty-five fighters. flak intense, heavy and accurate. Met the fighters just before bombs away and had them for twenty five minutes. Shot over two hundred rounds, hit an ME. 109 but did no damage. Our waist gunner knocked one down at 4:00 o'clock level. Our squadron destroyed four and a probable on one. Target well covered. 347th Sq. lost a ship. Sky was black with flak.

MISSION #23

DATE: JANUARY 11, 1944
TARGET: DOCKS AND SHIPPING
LOCATED: ATHENS, GREECE
SHIP: LEAD SHIP OF GROUP
NUMBER: 439
PILOT: COL. LAWRENCE
HOURS: 7:00
POSITION: LEFT WAIST

Hit a bad front just before target, did a 360 degree over Athens to reform group. Flak was intense, heavy and accurate. Met about thirty fighters and had them for thirty minutes. One ship in our squadron came home with over 400 holes. 346th Sq. lost a ship. Several of our ships shot up bad. Five fortresses collided and went down. One P-38 ran into another fortress and both went down in flames.

Flew waist position for Col. Lawrence on group crew today. We hit a large cloud formation at the coast of Albania on the Adriatic Sea. The whole group headed for the deck. Several planes scraped coming down through the clouds. I watched one tail gunner behind us hit the silk. His plane made it back ok. Tito's men picked him up and returned him to Italy for a fee.

My 50-Mission Diary

My 50-Mission Diary

23 RD MISSION
DATE - JAN. 11 13 1944
TARGET - DOCKS & SHIPPING
LOCATED - ATHENS, GREECE
SHIP - LEAD SHIP OF GROUP
NO. - 439
PILOT - COL. LAWERANCE
HRS. - 7:00
POSITION - LEFT, WAIST

Hit a bad front just before target. Did a 360° over Athens to reform group. Flak was intense, heavy and accurate. Met about thirty fighters and had them for thirty minutes. One ship in our squadron came home with over 400 holes. 346 sq. lost a ship. Several of our ships shot up bad. Five Forts collided and went down. One P38 ran into another Fort and both went down in flames.

I flew waist position for
Col. Lawrence on Group Crew
to-day.

We hit a large cloud formation
at the coast of Albania on the
Adriatic Sea. The whole group
headed for the deck. Several
planes scraped coming down
through the clouds. I
watched one tail gunner
behind us hit the silk.
His plane made it back
ok.

Tito's men picked him
up and returned him to
Italy for a fee.

Comments: Mission #23

It was not unusual when flying in such a tight formation that some of our planes would collide. This was usually caused by one of the planes getting hit by flak and the pilot not being able to control it. The term, "hitting the silk," means that the airman parachuted out of the plane. A few days later, we learned that the underground for Tito's Yugoslavian army picked him up and returned him to Italy for a fee.

Col. Charles W. Lawrence, who was our pilot on this mission, later became the commanding officer of the 15th Air Force. What an honor to fly with him!

Colonel Charles W. Lawrence was our pilot on Mission 23.

ORLANDOAN is the newest one-star general in the Mediterranean theater. Brig. Gen. Charles W. Lawrence is commander of a 15th Air Force Flying Fortress wing and recently headed a task force on the first American shuttle bombing mission to Russia. The 43-year-old general was graduated from West Point in 1923. His wife, Mrs. Katherine B. Lawrence, and three children live in Orlando.

MY 50-Mission Diary

MISSION #24

DATE: JANUARY 13, 1944
TARGET: AIR FIELD
LOCATED: GUIDONIA, ITALY
SHIP: ROBT. E. LEE (LEAD)
NUMBER: 482
PILOT: CAPT. SHAW
HOURS: 3:00
POSITION: TAIL GUNS

Some flak and about fifteen fighters. Did a good job on target.

Located approximately 15 miles northeast of Rome.

24TH MISSION

DATE - JAN. 13TH 1944

TARGET - AIR FIELD

LOCATED - GUIDONIA, ITALY

SHIP - ROBT. E. LEE   LEAD SQ.

NO. - 482

PILOT - CAPT. SHAW

HRS. - 3:00

POSITION - TAIL GUNS

Some flak and about fifteen fighters.

Did a good job on target.

Located approximately 15 miles northeast of Rome

MISSION #25

DATE: JANUARY 14, 1944
TARGET: AIR FIELD
LOCATED: MOSTAR, YUGOSLAVIA
SHIP: ROBT. E. LEE (LEAD GROUP)
NUMBER: 482
PILOT: MAJ. MAC
CO-PILOT: COL. LAWRENCE
HOURS: 4:00
POSITION: TAIL GUNS

Flak intense, heavy and very accurate. One piece came through and missed me by six inches. Was stopped by a round of ammunition in my track. One of the navigator's windows was knocked out. Target was destroyed.

The flak was so rough they bounced us all over the sky. I thought they had me when the piece hit under my knee. Gives you sort of a jolt to have your knee knocked off the track and then see a hole in the plane. I am keeping this piece of 88 and the round of ammunition to remember this mission.

Mostar is on the central coast of Yugoslavia about 25 miles inland.

My 25th mission today! Will start down the other side on my next one.

My 50-Mission Diary

25Th MISSION

DATE - JAN. 14Th 1944

TARGET - AIR FIELD

LOCATED - MOSTAR, YUGOSLOVIA

SHIP - ROBT. E LEE   LEAD GROUP

NO. - 482

PILOT - MAJ. MAC. - CO-PILOT COL. LAWERANCE

HRS. - 4:00

POSITION - TAIL GUNS.

Flak intence, heavy and very accurate. One piece come through and missed me by six inches. Was stopped by a round of ammunition in my track. One of the navigators windows was knocked out.

Target was destroyed. Flak was sure rough they bounced us all over the sky.

I thought they had me
when the piece let under
my knee. Give you sort of
a jolt to have your knee
knocked off the track and
then see a hole in the
plane. I'am keeping this
piece of 88 and the round
of amunition to remember
this mission.

Mostar is on the central
coast of Yugoslavia about
25 mile inland.

My 25th mission to day,
will start down the other
side on my next one.

My 50-Mission Diary

This track of bullets blocked this piece of 88 flak, saving my knee, and possibly my life.

MISSION #26

DATE: JANUARY 15, 1944
TARGET: MARSHALLING YARDS
LOCATED: AREZZO, ITALY
SHIP: TAIL-END-CHARLIE
NUMBER: 351
PILOT: LT. WEIRN
HOURS: 4:00
POSITION: RIGHT WAIST

No fighters, very little flak. Target leveled.

Our crew was not scheduled to fly today, so Carter and I went to the operations tent to see if we could get on the loading list with a crew that might be short. They had one opening. We flipped a coin. I won, and got a mission in. Carter went to town and on his way home he jumped on a trailer load of bombs. He slipped and fell under the wheels and crushed both legs. He is in the hospital at Foggia. His war days are over.

Arezzo is located in Central Italy just south of Florence.

My 50-Mission Diary

26TH MISSION
DATE - JAN. 15TH 1944
TARGET - MARSHALLING YARDS
LOCATED - AREZZO, ITALY
SHIP - TAIL-END-CHARLIE
NO. - 351
PILOT - LT. WEIRN
HRS. - 4:00
POSITION - RIGHT WAIST

No fighters, very little flak. Target leveled.

Our crew was not scheduled to fly to-day, so Carter and I went to the Operations tent to see if we could get on the loading list with a crew that might be short. They had one opening. We flipped a coin I won, and got in a mission

Comments: Mission #26

When I returned from this mission, I remember how devastated I was to hear about Carter. He was taken to a hospital in Foggia, and while he was there, the hospital was bombed, causing him even more injuries. When he was able to travel, he

Carter went to town and on his way home he jumped on the trailer load of bombs, slipped and fell under the wheels. Crushed both legs. He's in the hospital at Foggia, his war days are over.

Arezzo is located in central Italy just south of Florence.

was sent back to the States and discharged. I visited him several times after I returned home. He was in constant pain from his injuries and died not long after the War ended.

This is a B-17 ready for takeoff on an airstrip in North Africa.

MISSION #27

DATE: JANUARY 16, 1944
TARGET: AIR FIELD
LOCATED: VILLAORBA UDINE, ITALY
SHIP: ROBT. E. LEE   LEAD GROUP
NUMBER: 482
PILOT: MAJOR MAC
HOURS: 4:40
POSITION: TAIL GUNS

Some flak. Met six Libs as we came off target. They were being attacked by five ME-109's. Saw three 109's go down. One blew up in mid-air, one went into a dive and didn't pull out. The other one went down over the sea. The pilot bailed out. The libs came over to us for protection and one was shot down by our own men. Nine chutes came out of the ship before it went into the sea in flames.

We thought at first they were some of our own planes flown by Germans, as this had happened before. They have a few of our planes captured in flying condition. Sometimes they will try to join our formation then open up without warning. This particular plane that was shot down did not signal by radio or show the colors of the day. So I guess the boys in the rear were trigger happy.

27TH MISSION
DATE - JAN. 16TH 1944
TARGET - AIR FIELD
LOCATED - UDINE. ITALY
VILLAORBA
SHIP - ROBT. E LEE. LEAD GROUP
NO. - 482
PILOT - MAJ. MAC.
HRS. - 4:40
POSITION - TAIL GUNS

Some flak, met six Libs as we come off target. They were being attacked by five ME 109's. Saw three 109's go down. One blew up in mid-air. One went into a dive and didn't pull out. The other one went down over the sea. The pilot bailed out. The Libs came over to us for protection and one was shot down by our own men. Nine chutes come out of the ship befor it went into the sea in flames.

Comments: Mission #27

Someone questioned what I meant by "the color of the day." This was a code used to decide if the plane was really one of ours trying to join our formation or a plane that the Germans had captured. To show the color of the day, we would fire rockets of the color out the waist window. They would, in turn, return the correct color. If the correct color wasn't shown, we would

We thought at first they were some of our own planes flown by Germans, as this had happened before. They have a few of our planes captured in flying condition. Sometimes they will try to join our formations then open up without warning. This particular plane that was shot down did not signal by radio or show the colors for the day. So I guess the boys in the rear were trigger happy

assume they were Germans trying to join our formation and we would shoot them down.

A Junker 88 bomber sat in front of our tent at our "home" in Foggia, Italy.

MISSION #28

DATE: JANUARY 17, 1944
TARGET: MARSHALLING YARDS
LOCATED: PRATO, ITALY
SHIP: ROBT. E. LEE (LEAD)
NUMBER: 482
PILOT: COL. LAWRENCE
HOURS: 5:00
POSITION: RIGHT WAIST

Little flak. no fighters. We flew completely around front lines. Target leveled.

Flew waist for Col. Lawrence, led the group. I prefer the tail position. Certainly cold standing at those waist windows.

Prato is just west of Florence in Central Italy.

28 ᵀᴴ MISSION

DATE - JAN. 17ᵀᴴ 1944
TARGET - MARSHALLING YARDS
LOCATED - PRATO, ITALY
SHIP - ROBT. E. LEE   LEAD-GROUP
NO. - 482
PILOT - COL. LAWRENCE
HRS. - 5:00
POSITION - RIGHT WAIST

Little flak, no fighters.
Flew completely around
front lines.
Target leveled.

Flew waist for Col. Lawrence
led group. I prefer the tail
position. Certainly cold
standing at these open waist
windows. Prato is just
west of Florence in central
Italy.

MISSION #29

DATE: JANUARY 19, 1944
TARGET: AIR FIELD
LOCATED: CENTECELLE, ITALY
SHIP: ROBT. E. LEE (LEAD WING)
NUMBER: 482
PILOT: COL. LAWRENCE
HOURS: 4:00
POSITION: RIGHT & LEFT WAIST

Flew with Col. Lawrence as pilot, Col. Thurman as co-pilot, a Major as observer and Capt. Jones as navigator.

29TH MISSION
DATE - JAN. 19TH 1944
TARGET - AIR FIELD
LOCATED - CENTECELLE, ITALY
SHIP - ROBT. E. LEE. LEAD-WING
NO. - 482
PILOT - COL. LAWERANCE
HRS. - 4:00
POSITION - RIGHT & LEFT WAIST

Flew with Col. Lawerance as pilot, Col. Thurman as co-pilot, a Major as observer and Capt. Jones as navigator.

Comments: Mission #29

On this mission I had to man both waist positions. The other gunner was sick just before takeoff.

MISSION #30

DATE: JANUARY 20, 1944
TARGET: AIR FIELDS
LOCATED: CAMPIANO AIO, ITALY
(NEAR ROME)
SHIP: BAD PENNY
NUMBER: 509
PILOT: LT. PERRY
HOURS: 4:00
POSITION: RIGHT WAIST

No flak, no fighters, carried frags, target destroyed.

Our left wing-man had several frag bombs tangled and hanging out of his bomb-bay. He dropped out of formation and finally cut them loose.

30 TH MISSION

DATE - JAN. 20 TH 1944

TARGET - AIR FIELDS

LOCATED - NEAR ROME. ITALY
(CAMPIANO A/D.)

SHIP - BAD PENNY

NO. - 509

PILOT - LT. PERRY

HRS. - 4:00

POSITION - RIGHT WAIST

No flak, no fighters
Carried frags, target destroyed.
Our left wing man had
several frag bombs tangled
and hanging out of his bomb
bay. He dropped out of formation
and finally cut them loose.

MISSION #31

DATE: JANUARY 22, 1944
TARGET: AIR FIELD & M/Y
LOCATED: PONTERERA, ITALY
SHIP: ROBT. E. LEE   - LEAD GROUP
NUMBER: 482
PILOT: COL. LAWRENCE
HOURS: 5:00
POSITION: RIGHT WAIST

Flew around near Rome for an hour and a half trying to find a target open. Made a run on one city, but bomb-bay doors would not open, so we hit the marshalling yards and air field in the town next to it. No fighters, no flak.

Returning home we found ourselves directly over the new invasion south of Rome. It didn't take us long to get out of there. We were directly over the first day invasion of Anzio. Several Spitfires came up to get us out of there. Looking down through the holes in the clouds all you could see was ships.

31 ST MISSION

DATE - JAN. 22 ND 1944

TARGET - AIR FIELD & M/Y

LOCATED - PONTEDERA, ITALY

SHIP - ROBT. E. LEE LEAD-GROUP

NO. - 482

PILOT - COL. LAWERANCE

HRS. - 5:00

POSITION - RIGHT WAIST

Flew around near Rome
for an hour and a half trying
to find a target over. Made a
run on one city, but bomb
bay doors would not open, so
we hit the marshalling yards
and air field in the town
next to it. No fighters, no flak.
Returning home we found
ourselves directly over the new
invasion south of Rome. It didn't
take us long to get out of there.

We were directly over
the first day invasion
at Anjio, Several Spitfires
come up to get out of there
Looking down through holes
in the clouds all you
could see was ships.

My 50-Mission Diary

This photo was taken from our plane over the Alps as we were coming out of Southern Germany. It was a beautiful sight.

MISSION #32

DATE: JANUARY 27, 1944
TARGET: FLIGHT TO ENGLAND
LOCATED: BOBINGTON AIR FIELD
SHIP: SPOOFER
NUMBER: 522
PILOT: MAJ. MAC
HOURS: 10:20
POSITION: TAIL GUNS

Left Italy, arrived five hours later in Algiers. Spent the night, took off the next morning for Marrakech, French Morocco. Arrived five hours later. Stayed there two days and then took off for England. Arrived 10:20 mins later. Had a hard time getting down through clouds. Took a general, col. and a civilian to England on military business. Maj. Emerson flew as co-pilot. We flew over the Headquarters of the French Foreign Legion (Sidi-Bel-Abbes). Took a shower in the King of Morocco's Palace at Marrakech. It's now a U.S.O. club.

General Patton landed just behind us at Marrakech. We went over and looked at his plane a C-54. We had to wait two days for weather clearance for England, but he took off two hours later for the same destination.

A civilian brought two crates of large oranges out to our plane, one marked General Eisenhower and the other for the crew. He said he knew the General wouldn't get his if he didn't give us one also. We picked up two sacks of sandwiches for the flight, one spam and one turkey. I can still hear General Atkinson griping about those lousy spam sandwiches. You know who ate the turkey.

32 ND MISSION

DATE - JAN. 27 TH 1944
TARGET - FLIGHT TO ENGLAND
LOCATED - BOBINGTON AIRFIELD - NEAR LO
SHIP - SPOOFER
NO. - 522
PILOT - MAJ. MAC.
HRS. - 10:20
POSITION - TAIL GUNS

Left Italy, arrived five hours later in Algeria. Spent the night took off the next morning for Marrakech, French Morocco, arr five hours later. Staged there to days and then took off for England. Arrived 10:20 min. lat Had a hard time getting dow through clouds. Took a gener l., and a civilian to England on military business. Maj. Emerson flew as Co-Pilot.

(Sidi-Bel-Abbes)

Flew over the Headquarters
of the French Foreign Legion
Took a shower in the King of
Morroco's Palace at Marrakech
It's now a U.S.O. Club.
General Patton landed just
before us at Marrakech. We
went over and looked at his
plane a C54. We had to
wait two days for weather
clearance for England, but he
took off two hours later for
the same destination.
A civilian brought two crates
of large oranges out to our plane, one
marked for General Eisenhower and
the other for the crew. He said he knew
the General wouldn't get his if he didn't give
us one also. We picked up two
sacks of sandwiches for the flight
one Spam and one turkey. I can still
hear General Atkinson gripping about those
lousy spam sandwiches. You know - who
ate the turkey.

My 50-Mission Diary

I'm sitting atop the B-17, named Spoofer, that
we flew to England.

MISSION #33

DATE: FEBRUARY 9, 1944
TARGET: FLIGHT BACK TO ITALY
LOCATED: CADZ AIRFIELD - CASABLANCA
FRENCH MOROCCO
SHIP: SPOOFER
NUMBER: 522
PILOT: MAJ. MAC
HOURS: 8:20
POSITION: TAIL GUNS

Flew from Bobington to St. Morgans in two hours. Was cleared of England and took off for Casablanca at 1:00 a.m. Arrived 8:20 minutes later. Had dinner then left for Algiers, arriving 3 hours later. Spent the night and left the next morning for Bari, Italy. Arrived six hours later. Let the Col. off and then blew out the tail wheel tire. We took off anyway and made it back to our home base in one hour. Gave the mess hall a good buzz job and then landed in a sixty mile wind with no tail wheel tire and the bombardier as co-pilot.

We had almost two weeks in London on our own. Our home was 44 Cadogan Place, Knightsbridge. First night in London got caught in an air raid. The subways quit running at 10:00 PM, couldn't get a taxi, had to walk about two miles in the black-out asking directions, finally reached Knightsbridge at 2:00 a.m. I climbed to the 3rd floor of three buildings before I found my own room. They all look alike in a black-out. The Germans bombed every night we were there. I'll never forget sitting in the theater with the throbbing of German bombers overhead. We could feel the concussion of bombs hitting, still stayed and watched the show. Had a nice time, hope to return some day when the bombs are not dropping.

33 RD MISSION

DATE - FEB. 9 TH 1944
TARGET - FLIGHT BACK TO ITALY
LOCATED -   CADZ AIRFIELD CASABLANCA
                  FRENCH   MOROCCO
SHIP - SPOOFER
NO. - 522
PILOT - MAJ. MAC.
HRS. - 8:20
POSITION - TAIL GUNS

I flew from Bobington to St. Morgans in two hours. Was cleared of England and took off for Casablanca at 1:00 am. Arrived 8:20 min later. Had dinner then left for Algeria, arrived 3 hours later. Spent the night and left the next morning for Bari, Italy. Arrived six hours later. Let the Col. off and then blew out the tail wheel tire. We took off anyway and made it back to our home base in one hour. Gave the mess hall a good buzz job and then landed in a sixty mile wind with no tail wheel tire and the bombardier as co-pilot.

My 50-Mission Diary

We had almost two weeks in
London on our own. Our home
was 44 Cordoggan Place, Knights
Bridge. First night in London
got caught in an air raid. The
subways quit running at 10:00 PM,
couldn't get a taxi, had to walk
about two miles in the black-
out asking directions, finally
reached Knights Bridge at
2:00 AM. I climbed to the 3rd floor
of three buildings before I found
my own room. They all look alike
or in a black-out. The Germans
bombed every night we were there.
I'll never forget setting in theaters
with the throbbing of German
bombers overhead. We could feel
the concussion of bombs hitting
still stayed and watched the
show. Had a nice time, hope
to return some day when the
bombs are not dropping.

Comments: Missions #32 & #33

The missions that stand out so vividly in my mind are my 32nd and 33rd missions. These were not rough missions, but I felt it was an honor and a privilege to have been a part of them. We flew from Foggia, Italy, to London, England, for rest and relaxation and 14 days on our own.

While having our coffee following our January 16th mission, our pilot and commanding officer, Major David MacDonald, stopped to talk to the crew. He said that he had only two missions left to finish his 50. General Joseph H. Atkinson contacted him and requested that Major Mac and his crew fly him to England for a special meeting. (We were not aware of this, but it was a pre-invasion meeting.) Our crew was scheduled for R&R at the Isle of Capri, so Major Mac told us it was not mandatory, but if we agreed, we could go to England for 14 days R&R instead of the Isle of Capri. Because it would be necessary for us to man our guns along the coast of Spain, Portugal, and France, where the Germans patrolled, we would be credited for two missions; coming and going. It didn't take us long to accept his invitation. The members of our regular crew who accepted the invitation were: Lieutenant Donald T. Hemmingson, bombardier, Technical Sergeant Ross E. McKinney, radio man, Staff Sergeant Clarence L. Danielson, waist gunner, and myself, Staff Sergeant Albert C. Henke, tail gunner.

On January 27th (Mission #32), we loaded our bags into "Spoofer" #522, a nearly new B-17G. I had flown on this plane once before on a mission with Lieutenant George Perry and crew.

We left Foggia, Italy, and landed at Algiers, where we spent the first night. The next morning, we headed to Marrakech. Enroute we flew low over "Sidi-Bel-Abbes," the famous "French Foreign Legion." We were billeted in the King of Morocco's winter palace in Marrakech, which, during the War, was converted into a USO club. (The King resided in his palace in the Atlas mountains.) We took our showers in the basement of this building. We were grounded there for two days because of the weather, which gave us the opportunity to tour the city. We saw the Djemma el Fna Marketplace, famous for its entertainers, and watched as the natives played their flutes and put the vipers through their swaying paces.

As we landed at Marrakech, a large, new C-54 plane landed behind us. Our curiosity got the best of us, and we went over to look at it. The crew was very nice and invited us in to see it. Everything was fine until suddenly, an officer came up the steps. It was none other than General George S. Patton Jr., pearl-handled twin six shooters and all. I must have been standing just six feet from him, when he unloaded on the crew chief, "What are these men doing in here? Get this plane fueled. We are taking off for England as soon as possible!" This was the same General Patton who slapped the two soldiers in the hospital at Sicily. General Dwight Eisenhower had relieved him of his duties replacing him with General Omar Bradley. Eisenhower told Patton to report to England for reassignment. Patton was not a "happy camper." Although all of the other planes were grounded, Patton's plane took off.

That evening, as we took off for England, a B-24 took off just ahead of us. As we left the runway, their plane veered to the left. All four engines cut out. They crashed. All we could see was a ball of fire as we flew over them. This hit us pretty hard because, while spending our two days waiting for weather clearance, they were parked next to us and we became pretty well acquainted. They were a new B-24 crew, and all of them were killed.

Our flight plan was due east to the 12th Meridian then north to St. Morgan, the south port of entry into the United Kingdom of England. I thought this was going to be an easy mission, but there were times when things got very tense. The first incident

My 50-Mission Diary

occurred about three hours into the flight. I was in the radio room by General Atkinson, when he tapped me on the shoulder and pointed at the #2 engine. The cover on the fuel tank was not latched properly. The cap must have vibrated loose, allowing a steady stream of gas to siphon out to within three feet of sparks from the #2 engine. We alerted Ross McKinney, the radio operator, who contacted M/Sgt. Novac in the top turret. He immediately started transferring fuel out of that tank. I can remember General Atkinson remarking, "What in the hell am I doing here, I could have been retired!"

It was pretty quiet for the next seven hours until we reached St. Morgan. There we found ourselves looking down on a solid overcast sky, and our radio was malfunctioning. Soon two Spitfires arrived and escorted us to a hole in the clouds. When we saw rooftops, we knew what the low ceilings were in England in January. There was no problem landing when we reached the runway and taxied to a revetment. It was just daybreak. I was the first to roll out of the side waist door. A small step stool had been placed by the door. I slipped on the first step and sprawled to the ground. All I could see when I looked up were two rows of white leggings—the honor guard for the General.

We received a first-class breakfast at their mess hall and then received clearance for a very low-altitude flight to Bobbington Airdrome, 18 miles northwest of London. Due to the extremely low ceiling all the way, we had quite a view of equipment and material that was stockpiled for the War. There were tanks, trucks, jeeps, ammunition, fuel, food, and other supplies stacked solid on both sides of every highway, road, or lane. (I later learned that these stockpiles were in preparation for the D-Day invasion.)

We parked "Spoofer," and stayed over night in transit quarters. We spent most of the night outside watching the aerial display as London was receiving quite a blitz job that night. We could hear the sirens wailing and ack-ack guns firing. We even saw some planes go down in flames. I thought to myself, we're going to ride a train into London in the morning to spend two weeks R&R? They must be kidding!

When we arrived by train in London the next morning, we transferred to a subway to Knightsbridge Station, near Buckingham Palace. We then rode a truck to "Hans Crescent Club," and were assigned to 44 Cadogan Place for billets and all meals at the club.

While dodging bombs at night, we did get to see quite a bit of London during the 14 days; London Bridge, Big Ben, Picadilly Circus, Parliament, Trafalgar Square, Old Bailey, the Thames River and many more well-known sights. The one thing that impressed me so much was how the people in London endured the hardships of the War. I saw whole families sleeping on iron cots set up on subway platforms at every station. They slept there night after night, while sirens moaned and concussions of falling bombs shook the ground. After spending 14 nights there, I was almost thankful to return to Foggia to resume my missions.—At least we could sleep at night.

We reported back to our plane at Bobbington and took off February 9th (Mission #33) for Casablanca, Morocco, landing at Cazes Airdrome, where we spent the night. Then next day, we flew to Algiers for an overnight stop. Then, skimming the waves of the Mediterranean Sea, we landed at Bari, Italy, to let Colonel Bunch off. A tail-wheel tire blew out when we landed, but we took off anyway and made it back to our home base. Major Mac gave the mess tent a good buzz job and then landed in a 60-mile-an-hour wind with no tail-wheel tire. Lieutenant Don Hemmingson, our bombardier, was co-pilot.

I'll never forget our trip to London. What a great experience, plus credit for two missions!

My 50-Mission Diary

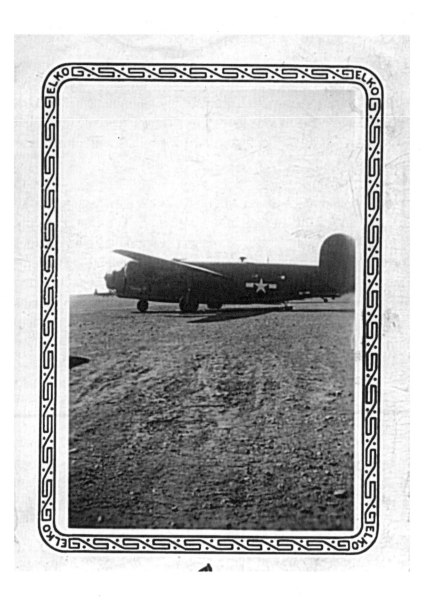

A new crew aboard this plane was headed for England, taking off from Marrakech. They crashed on takeoff just ahead of us. All were killed.

This is me in #522 Spoofer that we flew from Foggia, Italy, to London, England.

Staff Sergeant Clarence L. Danielson is atop #522 Spoofer.

MISSION #34

DATE: FEBRUARY 15, 1944
TARGET: GUNS AND TROOPS IN MONASTERY
LOCATED: CASSINO, ITALY
SHIP: FORT ALAMO II - LEAD SHIP
NUMBER: 696
PILOT: CAPT. SHAW
HOURS: 3:05
POSITION: TAIL GUNS

Target hit, no fighters some accurate flak. Could see the guns firing on front lines.

Major Mac finished his 50th on the England mission and will go home soon. Capt. Shaw will take over as commanding officer of our squadron. I am flying tail for him. I hate to see Mac leave but Capt. Shaw is a fine officer and a very good pilot.

Cassino is about half way between Naples and Rome. Coming back we flew about 100 feet high all of the way up the Volaturno River, sure a lot of fighting took place here. Burned out equipment all along the way.

34 TH MISSION
DATE - FEB. 15 TH 1944
TARGET - GUNS AND TROOPS IN MONISTERY
LOCATED - CASSINO, ITALY
SHIP - FORT ALAMO II   LEAD - SQ.
NO. - 696
PILOT - CAPT. SHAW
HRS. - 3:05
POSITION - TAIL GUNS

Target hit no fighters
some accurate flak.
Could see the guns firing
on front lines.
Major Mac finished his 50th
on the England mission and will
go home soon. Capt. Shaw
will take over as commanding
Officer of our squadron. I am
flying tail for him. I hate
to see Mac leave but Capt.

Shaw is a fine officer and
a very good pilot.

Cassino is about half way
between Naples and Rome.
Coming back we flew about
100 ft high all the way up
the Volaturno River, sure a
lot of fighting took place
here. Burned out equipment
all along the way.

Captain Burnham E. Shaw, Jr. became our new pilot and commanding officer.

MISSION #35

DATE: FEBRUARY 17, 1944
TARGET: TROOPS AND SUPPLIES
LOCATED: ANZIO, BEACHHEAD
SHIP: LADY LUCK
NUMBER: 507
PILOT: LT. SICKINGER
HOURS: 3:50
POSITION: RIGHT WAIST

Flak intense, heavy and accurate. One ship in our group knocked down. All the ships in our squadron were shot up pretty bad.

We went in at 13,000 feet and they turned their field pieces up at us. One 17 exploded, the tail assembly fluttered down to the beach and lit in a group of olive trees. Found out later the tail gunner was pinned in, and was knocked out, had two broken ribs, plenty lucky.

This mission was to help the men on the beachhead. The Germans were about to shove them back to the sea. We carried fragmentation bombs. I would have hated to see that brush pile falling from the sky on me.

35ᵀᴴ MISSION

DATE - FEB. 17ᵀᴴ 1944
TARGET - TROOPS AND SUPPLES
LOCATED - ANZIO, BEACHHEAD.
SHIP - LADY LUCK
NO. - 507
PILOT - LT. SICKINGER
HRS. - 3:50
POSITION - RIGHT WAIST.

Flak intense, heavy and accurate. One ship in our group knocked down. All the ships in our squadron were shot up pretty bad.
We went in at 13000 feet, and they turned their field pieces up at us. One 17 exploded, the tail assembly fluttered down to the beach and lit in a group of olive trees.

Found out later the tail gunner was pinned in, was knocked out, had two broken ribs, plenty lucky.

This mission was to help the men on the beach head. The Germans were about to shove them back to the sea. We carried fragmentation bombs. I would hated to see that brush pile falling from the sky on me.

When the brakes on this B-17 failed, it ended up in an olive field.

MISSIONS #36 & #37

DATE: FEBRUARY 22, 1944
TARGET: AIR CRAFT FACTORIES
LOCATED: REGENSBURG & AUGSBURG, GERMANY
SHIP: NEW MODIFIED "G" LEAD SQUADRON
NUMBER: 889
PILOT: CAPT. SHAW
CO-PILOT CAPT. MORRIS
HOURS: 6:55
POSITION: TAIL GUNS

My roughest raid so far. Started out with eight ships in our squadron, one turned back with engine trouble, four more turned back due to bad weather. Ended up over target with a right and left wing man. We were flying tail-end of the wing and was attacked by 35 ME-109's ME-210's. They hit our right wing man's left wing tank and he slid over us in flames and went down over the target. The left wing man was hit later and went down. We were the only one to return in our squadron. Our ship was shot up so bad it went to the bone yard. The top turret and radio gunner each shot down an ME-109. The ball turret and I knocked down an ME-210 a piece. I hit several others and fired 1,100 rounds of ammunition. Had a lot of trouble with the new tail turret. They sure threw the rockets at us today.

We lost 52 out of 177 bombers on this raid.

The armament major and a group of the Boeing factory men met me as I crawled out of the plane and were all excited about their new tail turret. I told them if they would saw off that tail and give me a shotgun I would feel safer. That was the one and only tail of that type.

COMBINDED WITH 8 TH AAF,
WE RECIVED CREDIT FOR 2 MISSIONS

36 TH
37 TH
MISSION

DATE - FEB. 22 ND, 1944
TARGET - AIR CRAFT FACTORYS
LOCATED - REGENSBURG & AUGSBURG GERMANY
SHIP - A NEW MODIFIED "G"   LEAD - SQUADRON
NO. - #889
PILOT - CAPT. SHAW - CAPT. MORRISS
HRS. - 6:55
POSITION - TAIL GUNS.

My roughest raid so far. started out with eight ships in our squadron, one turned back with engine trouble four more turned back due to bad weather. Ended up over target with a right and left wing man. We were flying tail-end of the wing and was attacked by 35 ME109 s and ME 210 s. They hit our right wing man's left wing tank and he slid over us in flames and went down over the target. The left wing man was hit later and

went down. We were the
only ones to return in our
squadron. Our ship was shot
up so bad it went to the bone
yard. The top turret and radio
gunner each shot down an ME. 109
The ball turret and I knocked
down an ME. 210 apiece.

I hit several others, fired
1100 rounds of ammunition.
Had alot of trouble with the
new tail turret.

They sure threw the rockets
at us to day.

We lost 52 out of 177
Bombers on this raid.

The Armament Major and a group of
Boeing factory men met me as I
crawled out of the plane and were all
excited about their new tail turret. I told
them if they would saw-off that tail and
give me a shot gun I would feel safer.
That was the one and only tail of that try.

ADVENTURES UNDER FIRE!

Comments: Missions #36 and #37

This was a combined raid with the 8th Air Force, so we received credit for two missions.

These missions were, by far, the roughest and most significant. (One year following these missions, General Nathan Twining said, "That was the turning point of the War in Europe.") I was proud to be a part of it and to have survived.

The following newspaper clippings and photos detail these missions. These missions are also described in greater detail in Chapter 9.

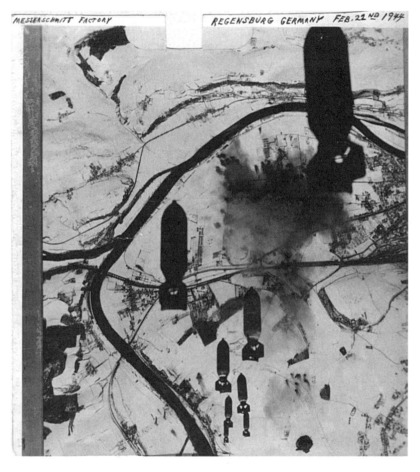

MESSERSCHMITT FACTORY   REGENSBURG GERMANY FEB.22 ND 1944

Bombs from our lead ship dropped on the Messerschmitt Factory target in Regensburg, Germany, on
February 22, 1944.

ADVENTURES UNDER FIRE!

TAR, WEDNESDAY, FEBRUARY 23, 1944.

FIERCE AIR FIGHT

U. S. Armadas From Britain and Italy Shoot Down 133 Nazi Fighters.

APART ON YANK LOSS

London Statement Says Toll Is 61 Bombers, but Mediterranean Reports 53.

British Capital Takes a Heavy Jolt in Night, but Ten Craft Are Bagged.

London, Feb. 23. (AP)—American bombers and fighters, striking powerfully from Britain and Italy in the first co-ordinated assault deep into Germany, crippled enemy aircraft production anew and knocked 133 Nazi fighter planes from the sky, United States army headquarters declared today.

Sixty-one big bombers were lost in yesterday's joint assault, which included diversionary raids by planes based in Italy, the announcement said. It listed forty-one bombers lost from the force attacking from Britain, and twenty missing from the U. S. 15th air force based in Italy.

Differ on Figures.

(Allied headquarters in the Mediterranean said only fifteen Italy-based planes were lost yesterday, and a spokesman said twelve were bombers. This would make the day's total bomber losses fifty-three.)

"In three days of record-breaking operations aimed at destroying Germany's capacity to maintain aerial resistance, American air force planes have accounted for 310 enemy fighters," headquarters said, with 153 falling to fighters of the 8th and 9th air forces in Britain, 117 destroyed by 8th air force bombers, and forty by 15th air force bombers.

The Germans threw up savage resistance as the Britain-based bombers struck the Junkers-88 assembly plant at Bernburg and aircraft and component factories at Aschersleben and Halberstadt. The 15th air force bombers from Italy blasted two Messerschmitt factories at Regensburg and bombed freight yards at Petershausen, twenty miles north of Munich.

Fierce Sky Battles.

Heavy bombers flying from Britain bagged thirty-four enemy fighters yesterday, and their escorts knocked down fifty-nine, while the bombers of the 15th air force destroyed forty Nazi craft.

South of Regensburg, Flying Fortresses engaged in a 55-minute battle with a score of ME-109s, ME210s and FW190s. Over the target, they were challenged by nine planes, and Staff Sergt. A. C. Henke, 8319 Morrell avenue, Kansas City, tail gunner, who destroyed an ME-210, said:

"Jerry came in on a level. I fired when he was way out, and stayed on the trigger. He finally broke away, smoking heavily, and fell beneath us."

A communique said that the 8th and 9th air forces lost eleven fighters yesterday, and that two fighters of the force in Italy were missing, for a total day's loss of seventy-four planes.

Today's German communique asserted 119 Allied planes, including ninety-five 4-engined bombers, were destroyed yesterday over Germany. Loss of sixty-one bombers over Germany Tuesday is a new record, since it is the first figure for combined operations from Britain and Italy of the United States strategic air force in Europe.

R. A. F. Mosquitoes maintained the offensive during the night, hitting unspecified targets in Western and Southwestern Germany without loss.

Blast at London.

A substantial number of German raiders made a 2-directional assault on London last night, showering high explosives and fire bombs over wide areas here and in other English sections, causing casualties, including at least ten killed, and starting fires in several districts.

Ten raiders were destroyed and anti-aircraft firepower hurled at the Germans from London at times was the greatest and most concentrated of the war, it was announced officially.

"Terrific barrages met the bombers who entered the metropolitan zone," a defense official said. "Many types of German planes, old and new, were identified and some used fresh tactics in trying to elude anti-aircraft concentrations and searchlights."

Several schools, including a famous one in the London area, were among the buildings wrecked.

An entire family of six was killed in one house. Next door three children were killed and another was injured. Several persons were injured in a village where several cottages were demolished.

This article appeared in the Kansas City Star. The following page features a clearer typed version of this original newspaper article.

FIERCE AIR FIGHT

U.S. Armadas from Britain and Italy Shoot Down 133 Nazi Fighters

APART ON YANK LOSS

London Statement Says Toll Is 61 Bombers, but Mediterranean Reports 53.

British Capital Takes a Heavy Jolt in Night, but Ten Craft Are Bagged.

London, Feb. 23, 1944 (AP)—American bombers and fighters, striking powerfully from Britain and Italy in the first coordinated assault deep into Germany, crippled enemy aircraft production anew and knocked 133 Nazi fighter planes from the sky, United States army headquarters declared today.

Sixty-one big bombers were lost in yesterday's joint assault, which included diversionary raids by planes based in Italy, the announcement said. It listed forty-one bombers lost from the force attacking from Britain, and twenty missing from the U.S. 15th air force based in Italy.

Differ on Figures.

(Allied headquarters in the Mediterranean said only fifteen Italy-based planes were lost yesterday, and a spokesman said twelve were bombers. This would make the day's total bomber losses fifty-three)

"In three days of record-breaking operations aimed at destroying Germany's capacity to maintain aerial resistance, American air force planes have accounted for 310 enemy fighters," headquarters said, with 153 fall-

ing to fighters of the 8th and 9th air forces in Britain, 117 destroyed by 8th air force bombers, and forty by 15th air force bombers.

The Germans threw up savage resistance as the Britain-based bombers struck the Junkers-88 assembly plant at Bernburg and air-frame and component factories at Aschersieben and Halberstadt. The 15th air force bombers from Italy blasted two Messerschmitt factories at Regensburg and bombed freight yards at Petershausen, twenty miles north of Munich.

Fierce Sky Battles.

Heavy bombers flying from Britain bagged thirty-four enemy fighters yesterday, and their escorts knocked down fifty-nine, while the bombers of the 15th air force destroyed forty Nazi craft.

South of Regensburg, Flying Fortresses engaged in a 55-minute battle with a score of ME-109s, ME-210s and FW-190s. Over the target, they were challenged by nine planes, and Staff Sgt. A. C. Henke, 8319 Morrell Avenue, Kansas City, tail gunner, who destroyed a ME-210, said:

"Jerry came in on a level. I fired when he was way out, and stayed on the trigger. He finally broke away, smoking heavily, and fell beneath us."

A communiqué said that the 8th and 9th air forces lost eleven fighters yesterday, and that two fighters of the force in Italy were missing, for a total day's loss of seventy-four planes.

Today's German communiqué asserted 119 Allied planes, including ninety-five 4-engined bombers, were destroyed yesterday over Germany.

Loss of sixty-one bombers over Germany Tuesday is a new record, since it is the first figure for combined operations from Britain and Italy of the United States strategic air force in Europe.

R.A.F. Mosquitoes maintained the offensive during the night, hitting unspecified targets in Western and Southwestern Germany without loss.

Blast at London.

A substantial number of German raiders made a 2-directional assault on London last night, showering high explosives and fire bombs over wide areas here and in other English sections, causing casualties, including at least ten killed, and starting fires in several districts.

Ten raiders were destroyed and anti-aircraft firepower hurled at the Germans from London at times was the greatest and most concentrated of the war, it was announced officially.

"Terrific barrages met the bombers who entered the metropolitan zone." A defense official said. "Many types of German planes, old and new, were identified and some used fresh tactics in trying to elude anti-aircraft concentrations and searchlights."

Several schools, including a famous one in the London area, were among the buildings wrecked.

An entire family of six was killed in one house. Next door three children were killed and another was injured. Several persons were injured in a village where several cottages were demolished.

My 50-Mission Diary

FEB 1945

AIR STRIDES IN A YEAR

DEADLY REGENSBURG BATTLE WITH LUFTWAFFE A LANDMARK.

In February, 1944, Fifty-Two Big Bombers of 177 Were Lost, Today Nine of 595 Are Downed by Flak.

BY HENRY J. TAYLOR.
(Scripps-Howard Special Correspondent.)

American Bomber Command Headquarters, Italy, Feb. 28.—With Maj. Gen. Nathan Twining at the controls of a Flying Fortress, I flew with him and his formation of nearly 1,000 planes, in a strike at Central Germany.

The mighty thrust demonstrated how far our airpower has progressed in one year, for this strike was made on the anniversary of the greatest air battle ever fought over Germany. That day, a year ago, the target was "impregnable" Regensburg. Today we flew over the same area, the target centering on Linz.

Over Regensburg, in February, 1944, we suffered the greatest losses ever inflicted on an American air force. It had been a planned effort to draw the luftwaffe fighter reserve out of hiding and break its back. At that time our fighters were based so far from Central Germany they did not have the range to get to the German fighters.

A 100-MINUTE BATTLE.

So our bombers had to meet them. They loaded each Fortress with 10,000 pounds of extra ammunition, and tackled the pride of the luftwaffe. From the Alps to Regensburg and back, the bombers battled 300 German fighters. We lost fifty-two bombers in 100 minutes; 390 American airmen were lost; 190 bailed out onto German soil.

But on the other side of the balance sheet, bombers tore the heart out of the luftwaffe reserve. Never again was the luftwaffe able to fight in such strength.

"That was the turning point of the air war in Europe," said General Twining.

Today's great attack showed the *DIFFERENCE IN ONE YEAR,*

kind of weather and using *the same route,* we flew in a formation *nearly* 100 miles long, an air train of *595* heavy bombers, escorted to the target and back by 334 fighters.

FLAK KNOCKS OUT NINE.

There were 6,284 Americans in the air on today's strike. Not one German fighter arose to attack. Instead of losing fifty-two bombers out of 177, we lost nine out of 595 (to flak). Instead of losing 580 men, we lost ninety. Instead of one climactic day's effort over Regensburg this is the thirteenth consecutive day General Twining's air force has put about 1,000 planes over German-held territory. The exact figure is 13,261 sorties in thirteen days.

Tonight General Twining had an anniversary celebration. His first word of praise was for the heroic men who did not come back from Regensburg. Then followed toasts: One to his 1st fighter group, the oldest in the air force; the second to the 82nd fighter group which holds a record for destroying 551 German planes in the air, plus 184 on the ground; the third to the 97th bombardment group for its record completion of 439 combat missions since it left England. The highlight of the celebration was a message from General H. H. Arnold, commanding general of the air forces.

FLAK IS MURDEROUS.

In the last year German antiaircraft fire has increased murderously in volume, concentration and accuracy. The fliers pay little attention to light flak, but the high, heavy stuff is fantastic to see. The usual notation on the operational blackboard says, "Heavy flak, intense, deadly."

As Hitler contracts his defense area, heavy 88 millimeter gun emplacements bristle anew around every target and multiply the problems of altitude and route for each raid.

The battle damage to the planes, requiring repairs and patching, burdens the daily operations to such a degree that accomplishing 1,000-plane raids daily is an immense *task* *Furt*hermore, the bombers *here fly* *from* widely scattered fields *instead* *of* the compact takeoffs in *Eng-* *land* and hence the rendezvous *re-* *quires* hours of planning and *extra* co-ordination of large groups of aircraft.

This article appeared in the Kansas City Star one year following the missions. The following page features a clearer typed version of this original newspaper article.

AIR STRIDES IN A YEAR

DEADLY REGENSBURG BATTLE WITH LUFTWAFFE A LANDMARK.

In February, 1944, Fifty-Two Big Bombers of 177 Were Lost, Today Nine of 595 Are Downed by Flak.

By Henry J. Taylor.
(Scripps-Howard Special Correspondent.)

American Bomber Command Headquarters, Italy, Feb. 28.—With Maj. Gen. Nathan Twining at the controls of a Flying Fortress, I flew with him and his formation of nearly 1,000 planes, in a strike at Central Germany.

The mighty thrust demonstrated how far our airpower has progressed in one year, for this strike was made on the anniversary of the greatest air battle ever fought over Germany. That day, a year ago, the target was "impregnable" Regensburg. Today we flew over the same area, the target centering on Linz.

Over Regensburg, in February, 1944, we suffered the greatest losses ever inflicted on an American air force. It had been a planned effort to draw the Luftwaffe fighter reserve out of hiding and break its back. At that time our fighters were based so far from Central Germany they did not have the range to get to the German fighters.

A 100-MINUTE BATTLE

So our bombers had to meet them. They loaded each Fortress with 10,000 pounds of extra ammunition and tackled the pride of the Luftwaffe. From the Alps to Regensburg and back, the bombers battled 300 German fighters. We lost fifty-two bombers in 100 minutes; 390 American airmen were lost; 190 bailed out onto German soil.

But on the other side of the balance sheet, bombers tore the heart out of the Luftwaffe reserve. Never again was the Luftwaffe able to fight in such strength.

"That was the turning point of the air war in Europe," said General Twining.

Today's great attack showed the kind of weather and using the same route, we flew in formation nearly 100 miles long, an air train of 595 heavy bombers, escorted to the target and back by 334 fighters.

FLAK KNOCKS OUT NINE.

There were 6,284 Americans in the air on today's strike. Not one German fighter arose to attack. Instead of losing fifty-two bombers out of 177, we lost nine out of 595 (to flak). Instead of losing 580 men, we lost ninety. Instead of one climactic day's effort over Regensburg this is the thirteenth consecutive day General Twining's air force has put about 1,000 planes over German-held territory. The exact figure is 13,261 sorties in thirteen days.

Tonight General Twining had an anniversary celebration. His first word of praise was for the heroic men who did not come back from Regensburg. Then followed toasts; One to his 1st fighter group, the oldest in the air force; the second to the 82nd fighter group which holds a record for destroying 551 German planes in the air, plus 184 on the ground; the third to the 97th bombardment group for its record completion of 439 combat missions since it left England. The highlight of the celebration was a message from General H. H. Arnold, commanding general of the air forces.

FLAK IS MURDEROUS

In the last year German anti-aircraft fire has increased murderously in volume, concentration and accuracy. The fliers pay little attention to light flak, but the high, heavy stuff is fantastic to see.

The usual notation on the operational blackboard says, "Heavy flak, intense, deadly."

As Hitler contracts his defense area, heavy 88 millimeter gun emplacements bristle anew around every target and multiply the problems of altitude and route for each raid.

The battle damage to the planes, requiring repairs and patching, burdens the daily operations to such a degree that accomplishing 1,000-plane raids daily is an immense task. Furthermore, the bombers here fly from widely scattered fields instead of the compact takeoffs in England and hence the rendezvous requires hours of planning and early co-ordination or large groups of aircraft.

NATHAN F. TWINING
Major General USA
Commanding 15th AAF

Major General Nathan F. Twining was quoted in an article appearing in the Kansas City Star a year later, saying, "That was the turning point of the air War in Europe."

MISSION #38

DATE: MARCH 2, 1944
TARGET: TROOPS
LOCATED: ANZIO BEACHHEAD
SHIP: ROBT. E. LEE
(LEAD SQUADRON)
NUMBER: 482
PILOT: CAPT. SHAW
CO-PILOT: CAPT. MORRIS
HOURS: 3:30
POSITION: TAIL GUNS

Flak was heavy intense and accurate. No fighters. Hit the beachhead again. Things are really hot up there.

38TH MISSION

DATE - MAR. 2ND 1944
TARGET - TROOPS.
LOCATED - ANZIO BEACHHEAD
SHIP - ROBT. E. LEE   LEAD - SQUADRON
NO. - 482
PILOT - CAPT. SHAW   CAPT. MORRISS
HRS. - 3:30
POSITION - TAIL GUNS

Flak was heavy, intense
and accurate, no fighters.
Hit the beachhead again,
things are really hot up
there.

MISSION #39

DATE: MARCH 3, 1944
TARGET: MARSHALLING YARDS
LOCATED: ROME, ITALY
SHIP: ROBT. E. LEE (LEAD SQUAD-RON)
NUMBER: 482
PILOTS: CAPT. SHAW
CAPT. MORRIS
HOURS: 4:30
POSITION: TAIL GUNS

Very little flak, six fighters but they did not attack.

Target leveled. Flew over the heart of Rome. Had a nice view of the Vatican City.

Capt. Shaw finished his missions today. He was promoted to Major and will leave for the states. He said he would call my mother and tell her I have only 11 more to go.

Major Morris will take over the squadron as Commander. I will be his tail gunner. He also was a pilot in Elliot Roosevelt's outfit.

39ᵀᴴ MISSION

DATE - MAR. 3ᴿᴰ 1944
TARGET - MARSHALLING YARDS
LOCATED - ROME, ITALY
SHIP - ROBT. E. LEE. LEAD SQ.
NO. - 482
PILOT - CAPT. SHAW   CAPT. MORRISS
HRS. - 4:30
POSITION - TAIL GUNS

Very little flak. six
fighters, but, they did not
attack.
    Target leveled.
Flew over the heart of
Rome. Had a nice view of
the Vatican City.
Capt. Shaw finished his missions
to day. Was promoted to Major
and will leave for the states.
He said he would call my

mother and tell her I have
only three more to go.
Major Morris will take over
the squadron as Commander,
I will be his tail gunner.
He also was a pilot in
Elliot Rossvelti outfit.

My 50-Mission Diary

Captain Burnham E Shaw, Jr. completed his 50th mission on March 3, 1944.

MISSION #40

DATE: MARCH 7, 1944
TARGET: SUBMARINE PENS
LOCATED: TOULON, FRANCE
SHIP: LEAD SHIP
NUMBER: 508
PILOT: MAJ. MORRIS
HOURS: 7:55
POSITION: TAIL GUNS

Had to turn back twenty-five minutes before the target due to bad weather. 301st group went through and hit target. Several ME-109's hit us out at sea and knocked one ship down. My heat suit, gloves and boots burned out and I just about froze to death. Was 45 degrees below zero and we were at altitude for seven hours.

One gunner in our squadron on his 50th mission was being congratulated over the intercom as we were attacked out at sea. He caught a 20 mm in the chest, blew him wide open.

40.TH MISSION
DATE - MAR. 7TH 1944
TARGET - SUBMARINE PENS
LOCATED - TOULON, FRANCE
SHIP - LEAD SHIP OF SQUADRON
NO. - 508
PILOT- MAJ. MORRISS
HRS. - 7:55
POSITION - TAIL GUNS

Had to turn back twenty-five minutes before the target due to bad weather. 301st group went through and hit target. Several ME.109s hit us out at sea and knocked one ship down. My heat suit, gloves and boots burned out and I just about froze to death.

Was 45 degrees below zero and we were at altitude for seven hours.

One gunner in our squadron
on his 50th mission was being
congratulated over the inter-com
as we were attacked out at sea.
He caught a 20 M.M. in the chest,
blew him wide open.

Italy: Hitch in Hell

I'm sitting here a thinkin' of what I left behind,
So I'll put it down in writin' what's runnin' through my mind.
We've dropped so many bloomin' bombs and done so many flights,
An' froze our feet an' hands an' things while at sub-zero heights.
But there is one consolation. Now you listen while I tell.
When we die, we'll go to heaven, cause we've done our hitch in hell.

We've taken a million Atabrine, those dirty yellow pills,
To fortify our systems agin' the fever an' the chills.
We've seen a million ack-ack bursts around us in the sky.
Fear gripped our hearts and chilled our blood when flak began to fly.
"Put on those lovin' flak suits," we hear our pilots yell,
"Cause this ain't a bloomin' picnic. It's another hitch in hell."

But when the taps have sounded, and we leave our earthly cares,
We'll stage our best parade of all, upon the Golden Stairs.
Angels will be there to meet us, and harps will softly play.
We'll draw a million dollars, and we'll spend it in a day.
Gabriel will be there to meet us, and St. Peter will proudly yell,
"Front seats, you guys from Italy. You've done your hitch in hell."

by Lt. Harry R. Hathaway
Killed in Action, February 22, 1945
348th Bomb Squadron – 99th Bomb Group

MISSION #41

DATE: MARCH 15, 1944
TARGET: TOWN PROPER
LOCATED: CASSINO, ITALY
SHIP: MISS PEGGY
NUMBER: 883
PILOT: LT. MUSKGROVE
HOURS: 3:05
POSITION: TAIL GUNS

No flak, no fighters, target leveled. Every available plane, heavy, light and fighter bombers pounded this target all day. We flew a morning mission, ate lunch on the line and was ready to take off again when they canceled out.

Got in an extra mission today, as our crew didn't fly—only nine to go.

41 ST MISSION

DATE- MAR. 15 TH 1944
TARGET - TOWN PROPER
LOCATED - CASSINO, ITALY
SHIP - MISS PEGGY
NO. - 883
PILOT - LT. MUSKGROVE
HRS. - 3:05
POSITION - TAIL GUNS.

No flak, no fighters
Target leveled.
Every available plane, Heavy,
light and fighter bombers
pounded this target all day.
We flew a morning mission
eat lunch on the line and
was ready to take off again
when they cancelled out.
Got in an extra mission
to-day as our crew didn't
fly, only nine to go.

MISSION #42

DATE: MARCH 17, 1944
TARGET: AIR CRAFT FACTORY
LOCATED: FISCHAMEND, AUSTRIA
(VIENNA)
SHIP: LEAD SHIP
NUMBER: 508
PILOT: MAJ. MORRIS
HOURS: 6:30
POSITION: TAIL GUNS

Had to turn back sixty miles from target, due to bad weather. Had a few fighters. They knocked down three Forts with rockets.

Forty-second mission, beginning to sweat them out a little. Didn't look like much chance of finishing, but beginning to see the end.

42ND MISSION
DATE - MAR. 17TH 1944
TARGET - AIR CRAFT FACTORY
SHIP - LEAD SHIP OF SQUADRON
NO - 508
PILOT - MAJ. MORRISS
LOCADED - FISCHAMEND. AUSTRIA
VIENNA
HRS. - 6:30
POSITION - TAIL GUNS.

Had to turn back sixty
miles from target, due to
bad weather. Had a few
fighters. They knocked
down three Forts with
rockets.
Forty-Second mission, beginning
to sweat them out a little
Didn't look like much chance
of finishing, but beginning
to see the end.

MISSION #43

DATE: MARCH 18, 1944
TARGET: AIR FIELD
LOCATED: UDINE, ITALY - VILLOARBA
A/D
SHIP: LEAD SHIP
NUMBER: 778
PILOT: MAJ. MORRIS
HOURS: 5:00
POSITION: TAIL GUNS

Attacked by sixty fighters, thirty minutes before target. Our P-47 escorts were intercepted. Saw five Forts explode behind us, hit by rockets. Five ships in our squadron were shot up bad. We destroyed 106 planes on the ground besides what was knocked out of the air. Received a commendation from General Twining.

Part of the 19th Bomb Group from the South Pacific flew with us today. This is the famous "Queen's Die Proudly" group. The Jerries sure picked on their new shinny planes. They lost their Squadron Commander and Operations Officer on this raid. This was certainly a cocky bunch. They came over to show us how to do the job.

My 50-Mission Diary

43RD MISSION

DATE - MAR. 18TH 1944

TARGET - AIR FIELD

LOCATED - UDINE, ITALY
VILLOARBA A/D

SHIP - LEAD SHIP OF SQUADRON

NO. - 778

PILOT - MAJ. MORRISS

HRS. - 5:00

POSITION - TAIL GUNS.

Attacked by sixty fighters
thirty minutes before target. Our
P47 escorts were intercepted. Saw
five Forts explode behind us,
hit by rockets. Five ships in
our squadron were shot up bad.
We destroyed 106 planes on the ground
besides what was knocked out of the
air. Received a commendation
from Gen. Twining,
Part of the 19th Bomb Group

My 50-Mission Diary

from the South Pacific, flew
with us to-day. This is the
famous "Queen's Die Moddly"
Group. The Jerries sure picked
on their new shiny planes.
They lost their Squadron
Commander and Operations Officer
on this raid.

They are Certainly a
cocky bunch. They came
over to show us how to
do the job.

My 50-Mission Diary

Several B-17s getting ready for takeoff for a mission.

MISSION #44

DATE: MARCH 19, 1944
TARGET: AIRCRAFT FACTORY
LOCATED: KLAGENFURT, AUSTRIA
SHIP: LEAD SHIP
NUMBER: 508
PILOT: MAJ. MORRIS
HOURS: 6:00
POSITION: TAIL GUNS

Attacked by sixty fighters. Saw four Forts go down in flames, hit by rockets. One Lib knocked down over target by flak. Hit target. P-38's had a real dog fight.

Klagenfurt is on the southern border of Austria. We sure passed over a lot of enemy fighter strips on this run.

My 50-Mission Diary

44 <u>Th</u> MISSION

DATE - MAR. 19 <u>Th</u> 1944
TARGET - AIR CRAFT FACTORY
LOCATED - KLAGENFUAT, AUSTRIA
SHIP - LEAD SHIP OF SQUADRON
NO. - 508
PILOT - MAJ. MORRISS
HRS - 6:00
POSITION - TAIL GUNS

 Attacked by sixty fighters.
Saw four Forts go down in
flames, hit by rockets. One
Lib knocked down over target
by flak.
 Hit target.
P 38's had a real dog-fight.
Klagenfurt is on the southern
border of Austria. We sure
passed over a lot of enemy
fighter strips on this run.

MISSION #45

DATE: MARCH 22, 1944
TARGET: MARSHALLING YARDS
LOCATED: VERONA, ITALY
SHIP: LEAD SHIP
NUMBER: 438
PILOT: MAJ. MORRIS
HOURS: 7:00
POSITION: TAIL GUNS

Met a few fighters, flak heavy, intense and accurate. Bucked a head wind all the way up, and went over target less than one hundred miles per hour. One Fort went down over target hit by flak.

Once we dropped our bombs the Maj. put her in a dive and with that tail wind we sure made good time getting back to the base. That old fortress rattled like a Model-T Ford.

Verona is near Lake Garda just west of Venice.

45TH MISSION

DATE - MAR. 22ND 1944
TARGET - MARSHALLING YARDS
LOCATED - VERONA, ITALY
SHIP - LEAD SHIP OF SQUADRON
NO. - 438
PILOT - MAJ. MORRISS
HRS. - 7:00
POSITION - TAIL GUNS

Met a few fighters, flak
heavy, intense and accurate.
Bucked a head wind all the
way up, and went over target
less then one-hundred miles
per hour. One Fort went down
over target, hit by flak.
Once we dropped our bombs
the Maj. put her in a dive
and with that tail wind we
sure made good time getting

back to the base. That
old fortress rattled like
a Model T Ford.
Verona is near Lake Garda
just West of Venice.

ADVENTURES UNDER FIRE!

While flying into incoming flak, a B-17 drops its bomb load.

MISSION #46

DATE: MARCH 28, 1944
TARGET: MARSHALLING YARDS
LOCATED: VERONA, ITALY
SHIP: ROBT. E. LEE
LEAD SQUADRON
NUMBER: 482
PILOT: MAJ. MORRIS
HOURS: 5:30
POSITION: TAIL GUNS

A few fighters, flak was heavy intense and accurate. Target was leveled. We picked up twelve holes in our ship. One just above my head.

Had to return to Verona to finish the job. They sure had the flak guns waiting for us.

46 TH MISSION
DATE - MAR. 28 TH 1944
TARGET - MARSHALLING YARDS
LOCATED - VERONA
SHIP - ROBT. E. LEE.   LEAD - SQUADN.
NO. - 482
PILOT - MAJ. MORRISS
HRS. - 5:30
POSITION - TAIL GUNS

A few fighters, flak was heavy, intense and accurate. Target was leveled.
We picked up twelve holes in our ship. One just above my head.
Had to return to Verona to finish the job. They sure had the flak guns waiting for us.

Comments: Mission #46

When we returned to base after this mission and I saw all of the holes in the plane, I couldn't believe we made it. The bullet hole just above my head really made me think that God was with me that day and perhaps I might get to finish my 50 missions and return home.

MISSION #47

DATE: MARCH 29, 1944
TARGET: MARSHALLING YARDS
LOCATED: TURIN, ITALY
SHIP: ROBT. E. LEE
(LEAD SQUADRON)
NUMBER: 482
PILOT: MAJOR MORRIS
HOURS: 7:15
POSITION: TAIL GUNS

Six fighters, flak heavy, moderate and accurate. Target leveled. We lost one Fort.

A beautiful sight of Switzerland again, one plane in our group was on fire over the target. They peeled off and headed for the promised land.

47 Th MISSION
DATE - MAR. 29 Th 1944
TARGET - MARSHALLING YARDS
LOCATED - TURIN, ITALY
SHIP - ROBT. E. LEE   LEAD-SQUADRON
NO - 482
PILOT - MAJ. MORRISS
HRS. - 7:15
POSITION - TAIL GUNS

Six fighters. flak heavy,
moderate and accurate.
Target leveled.
We lost one Fort.
A beautiful sight of
Switzerland again, one plane
in our group was on fire
over the target, they pulled
off and headed for the
promised land.

MISSION #48

DATE: MARCH 30, 1944
TARGET: GERMAN HEADQUARTERS
-CITY PROPER
LOCATED: SOFIA, BULGARIA
SHIP: FORT ALAMO II
NUMBER: 696
PILOT: LT. CARROLL
HOURS: 6:00
POSITION: TAIL GUNS

Quite a bit of flak, about ten fighters. We missed target but the other groups leveled the heart of the city.

We always worry about going down in Bulgaria, the civilians have a habit of meeting you with a pitch fork before you hit the ground. They don't believe in taking prisoners.

My 50-Mission Diary

48Th MISSION
DATE - MAR. 30Th 1944
TARGET - GERMAN HEADQUARTERS - CITY PROPER
LOCATED - SOFIA, BULGARIA
SHIP - FORT ALAMO II
NO. - 696
HRS - 6:00
POSITION - TAIL GUNS
PILOT - LT. CARROLL

Quite a bit of flak. about ten fighters. We missed target but the other groups leveled the heart of the city. We always worry about going down in Bulgaria, the civilians have a habit of meeting you with a pitch fork before you hit the ground. They don't believe in taking prisoners.

MISSIONS #49 & #50

DATE: APRIL 2, 1944
TARGET: AIRCRAFT FACTORY, BALL
BEARINGS & MARSHALLING
YARDS LOCATED: STEYR,
AUSTRIA
SHIP: LEAD SQUADRON
NUMBER: 074
PILOT: MAJOR MORRIS
CO-PILOT: CAPT. CARROLL
HOURS: 7:05
POSITION: TAIL GUNS

Had close to 300 enemy fighters off and on for about two & a half hours. There were JU-88's, ME-109's, ME-210's, ME-110's, FW-190's, JU-87's, and even some four engine ME-410's. Flak was heavy, intense and accurate. We lost two ships out of our squadron. The sky was black with flak, rockets and fighters. We lost 51 bombers and destroyed 129 fighters.

Due to a new Commanding General's orders that no credit would be given unless bombs were dropped on the target it took four flights to get my last mission in. We would climb 31,000 feet trying to get over the solid front, had flak and fighters, and still no credit. Capt. Carroll flew as our co-pilot and had to watch his regular crew go down over the target.

I was certainly happy to hear upon landing

My 50-Mission Diary

that we received credit for two missions because this was a combined raid with the 8th Air Force. I didn't know I had finished up until the ground crew told me when we landed.

THE END. THANK GOD!

Comments: Missions #49 & #50

When our crew Chief, Pete Bezek, told me I had completed my 50 missions, I about lost it. Everyone dreaded that last mission and to think I had completed mine was music to my ears. Now all I had to do was to prepare for the trip home.

My 50-Mission Diary

WAR DEPARTMENT
AAF FORM NO. 5
APPROVED DEC. 7, 1942

INDIVIDUAL FLIGHT RECORD

(1)SERIAL NO.   (2)NAME **HENKE,**   **Albert**   **C.**   (3)RANK **S/Sgt**   (4)AGE

(5)PERS. CLASS **20**   (6)BRANCH **Air Corps**   (7)STATION **APO 520**

ORGANIZATION ASSIGNED **15th**   **5th**   **99th**   **416th**

(9)ORGANIZATION ATTACHED

(10)PRESENT RATING & DATE   (11)ORIGINAL RATING & DATE

(12)TRANSFERRED FROM   (13)FLIGHT RESTRICTIONS

(15)TRANSFERRED TO **APO 520**   (14)TRANSFER DATE

(16) DO NOT WRITE IN THIS SPACE

PERS. CLASS	RANK	RTG.	A.F.	COMMAND	WING	GROUP NO.	TYPE	SQUADRON NO.	TYPE	STATION	MO.	YR.	(17) MONTH
													April 1944

DAY 18	AIRCRAFT TYPE, MODEL & SERIES 19	NO. LANDINGS 20	FLYING INST (INCL IN 1ST PIL TIME) S 21	COMMD. PILOT C CA 22	CO- PILOT CP 23	QUALI- FIED PILOT DUAL QD 24	FIRST PILOT DAY 25	FIRST PILOT NIGHT P N OR N 26	RATED PERS. NON-PILOT 27	28	NON-RATED 29	OTHER ARMS & SERVICES 30	OTHER CREW & PASS OR Q 31	INSTRU- MENT. 32	NIGHT N 33	INSTRU- MENT TRAINER 34	PILOT NON-ML AIRCRAFT OVER 400 H.P. 35	UNDER 400 H.P. 36
2	B17G	1											7:45					
16	B17G	1											1:00					

CLOSED: CHANGE OF STATION
CERTIFIED CORRECT:

Charles K. Carroll
CHARLES K. CARROLL
1st Lt AC
Asst Operations Officer

COLUMN TOTALS

	(42) TOTAL STUDENT PILOT TIME	(43) TOTAL FIRST PILOT TIME	(44) TOTAL PILOT TIME
(37) THIS MONTH			
(38) PREVIOUS MONTHS THIS F. Y.			
(39) THIS FISCAL YEAR			
(40) PREVIOUS FISCAL YEARS			
(41) TO DATE			

AIRCRAFT	NL	CARD NO. 1						CARD NO. 2					CARD NO. 3			
19	20	21	22	23	24	25	26	27	28	29	30	31	32	33	34	35	36

This is a copy of my orders, or the Individual Flight Record, of my last mission.

50-MISSION LOG

This is the actual certified copy of my mission log. (Since the actual mission log may be difficult to read, I have also included a transcribed version.) We received credit for two missions if we flew a combined raid with the 8th Air Force. However, there were other times that we flew and were not credited for the mission because the target was obscured by clouds that prevented us from dropping bombs. (This explains why there are a few discrepancies between diary entries and this verified mission log.)

FOUR HUNDRED SIXTEENTH
BOMBARDMENT SQUADRON (H)
Office of the Operations Officer

"This is to certify that HENKE, Albert C S/Sgt. has completed the following fifty (50) missions and total hours:"

PLANE	#	MISSION #	PILOT	TARGET	DATE	HOURS	POSITION
Widow Maker	244	1	Lt. Wilson	Benevento, Italy	16-Sep-43	5.35	Tail
Bad Penny	509	2	Lt. Bioggio	Viterbo, Italy	18-Sep-43	6.00	Waist
Sweater Girl	472	3	Lt. Trentadue	Pisa, Italy M/Y	4-Oct-43	6.20	Waist
Miss Peggy	883	4	Capt. Buck	Bologna, Italy M/Y	5-Oct-43	7.25	Ball
Lead Ship of Squad	471	5	Capt. Buck	Salonika, Greece	9-Oct-43	9.05	Ball
Miss Peggy	883	6	Capt. Buck	Terni, Italy M/Y	14-Oct-43	6.10	Ball
Lady Luck	507	7	Lt. Beaur	Genoa, Italy M/Y	29-Oct-43	7.35	Ball
Lady Luck	507	8	Lt. Beaur	Turin, Italy M/Y	30-Oct-43	5.45	Ball
Smiley	244	9	Lt. Borman	Wiener Neustadt, Austrla A/C Fact.	2-Nov-43	11.20	Waist
Lady Luck	507	10	Capt. Shaw	Turin, Italy	8-Nov-43	6.35	Tail

PLANE	#	MISSION #	PILOT	TARGET	DATE	HOURS	POSITION
Lead Ship of Squad	471	11	Maj. MacDonald	Bolzano, Italy M/Y & RR Bridge	10-Nov-43	9.00	Tail
Robert E. Lee (Lead Wing)	482	12	Maj. MacDonald & Gen. Ackinson	Toulon, France Sub Base	24-Nov-43	6.50	Tail
Robert E. Lee (Lead)	482	13	Maj. MacDonald	Fiano Romano, Italy L/G	29-Nov-43	6.40	Tail
Robert E. Lee (Lead)	482	14	Maj. MacDonald	Athens, Greece A/D & Piraeus Harbor	14-Dec-43	6.05	Tail
Robert E. Lee (Lead)	482	15	Maj. MacDonald	Innsbruck, Austria M/Y	19-Dec-43	6.00	Tail
Fort Alamo II (Lead)	696	16	Capt. Shaw	Udine, Italy M/Y	25-Dec-43	4.40	Tail
88%	696	17	Capt. Shaw	Rimini, Italy M/Y	28-Dec-43	4.35	Tail
Spoofer	522	18	Maj. MacDonald	Sofia, Bulgaria	4-Jan-44	6.35	Tail
Sweater Girl	472	19	Capt. Shaw	Maribor, Yugoslavia A/C Fact.	7-Jan-44	5.30	Tail
Robert E. Lee (Lead)	482	20	Capt. Shaw	Reggio Emilia, Italy A/C Fact.	8-Jan-44	5.35	Tail
Robert E. Lee (Lead)	482	21	Maj. MacDonald	Pola, Yugoslavia Harbor	9-Jan-44	3.50	Tail
Robert E. Lee (Lead)	482	22	Capt. Shaw	Sofia, Bulgaria	10-Jan-44	6.05	Tail
Lead Ship of Squad	439	23	Col. Lawrence	Piraeus, Greece Harbor & Halon Basin	11-Jan-44	7.00	Waist

My 50-Mission Diary

PLANE	#	MISSION #	PILOT	TARGET	DATE	HOURS	POSITION
Robert E. Lee (Lead)	482	24	Capt. Shaw	Rome, italy Guidonia A/D	13-Jan-44	4.25	Tail
Robert E. Lee (Lead)	482	25	Maj. MacDonald & Col. Lawrence	Mostar, Yugoslavia A/D	14-Jan-44	4.00	Tail
Tail End Charlie	351	26	Lt. Weirn	Arezzo, Italy M/Y	15-Jan-44	5.05	Waist
Robert E. Lee (Lead)	482	27	Maj. MacDonald	Villaorba, Italy M/Y	16-Jan-44	5.25	Tail
Robert E. Lee (Lead)	482	28	Col. Lawrence	Prato, Italy M/Y	17-Jan-44	5.25	Waist
Robert E. Lee (Lead)	482	29	Capt. Shaw	Rome, Italy Centocelle A/D	19-Jan-44	4.20	Waist
Bad Penny	509	30	Lt. Perry	Rome, Italy Ciampino A/D	20-Jan-44	4.05	Waist
Robert E. Lee (Lead Wing)	482	31	Col. Lawrence	Pontedera, Italy A/D	22-Jan-44	5.20	Waist
Fort Alamo II	696	32	Capt. Shaw	London, England	15-Feb-44	3.05	Tail
Lady Luck	507	33	Lt. Sickinger	Prato, Italy M/Y	17-Jan-44	3.50	Waist
New Modified "G" (Lead)	889	34/35	Capt Shaw & Capt. Morris	Regensburg, Germany	22-Feb-44	6.55	Tail
Robert E. Lee (Lead)	482	36	Capt. Shaw & Capt. Morris	Troops Beachead, Italy	2-Mar-44	4.15	Tail
Robert E. Lee (Lead)	482	37	Capt. Shaw & Capt. Morris	Rome, Italy Littorio M/Y	3-Mar-44	4.50	Tail

PLANE	#	MISSION #	PILOT	TARGET	DATE	HOURS	POSITION
Lead Ship of Squad	508	38	Maj. Morris	Anzio, Italy	7-Mar-44	7.35	Tail
Miss Peggy	883	39	Lt. Muskgrove	Cassino, Italy	15-Mar-44	8.05	Tail
Lead Ship of Squad	508	40	Maj. Morris	Vienna, Austria	17-Mar-44	6.00	Tail
Lead Ship of Squad	778	41	Maj. Morris	Villaorba, Italy A/D	18-Mar-44	5.20	Tail
Spoofer	522	42	Maj. MacDonald & Gen. Atkinson	Marrakech, Morroco St. Morgan, England	27-Jan-43	10.20	Tail
Spoofer	522	43	Maj. MacDonald	London, England - Casablanca, Italy	29-Jan-43	8.10	Tail
Lead Ship of Squad	508	44	Maj. Morris	Klagenfurt, Austria A/D	19-Mar-44	5.45	Tail
Lead Ship of Squad	438	45	Maj. Morris	Verona, Italy M/Y	22-Mar-44	6.00	Tail
Robert E. Lee (Lead)	482	46	Maj. Morris	Verona, Italy M/Y	28-Mar-44	5.30	Tail
Robert E. Lee (Lead)	482	47	Maj. Morris	Turin, Italy M/Y	29-Mar-44	7.05	Tail
Fort Alamo II	696	48	Lt. Carroll	Sofia, Bulgaria	30-Mar-44	5.45	Tail
Lead Ship of Squad	074	49/50	Maj. Morris & Capt. Carroll	Steyr, Austria	2-Apr-44	7.05	Tail
						286.75	

My World War II
Tour of Duty

Enlisted November 6, 1942

Fort Leavenworth—Leavenworth, Kansas

Sloan Field—Midland, Texas

Buckley Field—Aurora, Colorado

Army Air Corps Gunnery School—Las Vegas, Nevada

Boardwalk—Atlantic City, New Jersey

Camp Patrick Henry—Newport News, Virginia

Cazes Airdrome—Casablanca, French Morocco

Tunis, Tunisia

Foggia, Italy

Bobbington Airdrome—England

Knightsbridge—London, England

Foggia, Italy

Repel Depot—Naples Italy

Camp Kilmer—New Jersey

Jefferson Barracks—St. Louis, Missouri

Newport Air Base—Newport Arkansas

Home—Kansas City, Missouri

Miami Beach, Florida

Rattlesnake Air Base—Pyote, Texas

Fort Leavenworth—Leavenworth, Kansas

Discharged September 12, 1945

My World War II journey took me to many places, from enlistment through discharge.

Chapter

Other Memories

(Note: This chapter includes accounts not necessarily tied to any specific missions covered in Chapter 5. However, they stand out in my memory during my service overseas as I completed my missions.)

An Unexpected Reunion: Memory of Vernon Wells

In the fall of 1943, several B-24 Liberator Bombers landed at our base. Someone told me they were a squadron from the 8th Air Force stationed in England. They had just completed a mission on the Polesti Oil Fields. Polesti was farther from England than it was to our base, so they landed at our base for some repairs before returning to their home base in England.

When I was in the chow line, I met one of the crew from England and just to make conversation, I asked if he happened to know Vernon Wells. He said, "Well, yes. He is over in that tent across the road." I couldn't believe it! Talk about a needle-in-a-haystack. (Wells was one of my good buddies from gunnery school.) I ran to tell Dan Ives and the two of us went to Wells' tent. What a reunion we had! It was almost like getting a furlough home. Wells was on our base for about two weeks. We exchanged accounts of how conditions were in England and North Africa and what we had heard from home. We hated to say goodbye when they left to return to England.

Barbecue: Memory of General Doolittle's Speech

My eighth mission was to Turin, Italy, on October 30, 1943. This is when the 99th Bomb Group completed their 100th mission. General James Doolittle flew in to help celebrate this milestone. (The 99th Bomb Group flew 395 combat missions during World War II.) The 12th Air Force had just recently been renamed the 15th Air Force. Although it was a rainy day, the 99th had a barbecue and beer party for the men to celebrate the occasion. I was really feeling homesick about this time. I had just heard that one of our gunners was killed. He was in my class at gunnery school. I attended the party and will never forget General Doolittle's speech that night. I was sitting right up front, probably six feet from the General. He told us that America was now in a position to become more aggressive with the enemy and the air-War would be accelerated. Our job would be to knock out Hitler's Air Force, factories, oil fields, and marshalling yards. This would, in effect, cripple the Luftwaffe (the German Air Force).

It seemed from that day forward, our missions became longer and more dangerous. The fighters and flak were much more intense. As I said previously, I really didn't expect I would ever see home again so I might as well do the best job I could and hope for the best. As it turned out, I was one of the lucky ones who completed 50 combat missions and survived.

General James Doolittle flew in to celebrate the completion of the 100th Mission for the 99th Bomb Group. We enjoyed a barbecue and speech from General Doolittle.

ADVENTURES UNDER FIRE!

Living with the Crew:
Memory of Gene Canciglia

The men in our crew were a good-natured group of guys. This was a real bonus because we had to depend on each other so much. The six crew members, with the exception of the officers, shared the same tent so we were lucky to have such a congenial group.

Gene Canciglia, our engineer/gunner was a little older than the rest of us. He had joined the Air Force before the War and was a dedicated, take-charge person whom I really respected. Gene had taken pilot training and was just about to get his wings when he was in an accident that left him with a broken leg. He was washed out of pilot training and later trained to be an engineer. Gene kept us all in line as far as keeping the tent and our plane clean and in ship-shape. He had a good sense of humor and was well-liked.

Phillip Wojack, the ball turret gunner, made a crude make-shift desk in which he kept his personal belongings. Practically every time Gene came into the tent, he would trip on the leg of this "desk." He told Wojack the desk had to go, but Wojack was not ready to give it up. He told Gene, "The day I finish my missions, I don't care what you do to it." So the day Wojack completed his missions, and before he got off the truck, Gene took an axe to the desk and demolished it.

Soon after I joined the crew, Gene told me, "Partner, you don't have enough ammo here in the tail. If we rearranged this, we could put twice the ammo back here and you will probably need it." He asked how much I weighed. When I told him, he said, "I don't think the Major will even notice the drag." I remember there were several missions when that extra ammunition came in handy. I learned early on that if Gene made a suggestion, I should listen.

I do believe that one of the reasons we survived these missions was luck, but I think the main reason was that we had such an intelligent, reliable crew. There were no glory hounds aboard, everyone just did his job.

Our home away from home.

Phillip Wojack in the ball turret of a
B-17.

This picture shows Gene Canciglia destroying
Phillip Wojack's desk.

To the Rescue Again:
Memory of Dan Ives

Although Dan Ives was not a member of our regular crew, on one mission he flew with us as our ball turret gunner. Clarence Danielson was the right-waist gunner. For some unknown reason, Danielson's oxygen became unplugged and he passed out. When Ives tried to rotate the ball turret, he kept hearing a thump. Ives climbed up into the plane to see what was causing the noise and found Danielson, who by this time was turning blue. He quickly reconnected the oxygen and Danielson was revived.

This reminded me of when Ives saved my life in North Africa. (See Chapter 4—The Trip Overseas and Across North Africa.)

Daniel Ives proved to be a hero on more than one occasion. We served together from basic training to debarkation.

Clarence Danielson was a right-waist gunner on our crew.

V-Mails: Memories That Did and Didn't Make It Home

We didn't have the luxury of e-mails during World War II, and our mail service was really slow. It normally took from three to five weeks for letters to arrive at their destination. I suppose this was due to the huge volume of mail going back and forth. It boggles my mind to hear that our military today can e-mail their families in seconds. It was 90 days after I had completed my missions that I arrived home. My family didn't know whether I was dead or alive. Mom checked with the VFW and was told that they could not divulge this information, but that she would hear from the State Department if anything happened to me.

Instead of e-mail we had V-Mail. V-Mail was written on a V-Mail form and then, after the office at headquarters censored the contents, it was micro-filmed and sent to the States. When it arrived in the States, it was developed and sent on to its destination. My mother, bless her, saved all of my letters, which proved to be a valuable resource in writing this book. Our letters were censored from the time we arrived at the camp for debarkation overseas until we returned back in the States. If a letter was sent V-Mail, they assured us, it would reach its destination much faster. V-Mails were only a one-page letter. Of course, there was not a lot you could write home about anyway. (We were not allowed to say where we were or give details about missions. If we did, the censors "edited" the letters either by blacking out portions of the letter or actually cutting them out before they were sent.) I am including a few of these V-Mails so younger generations can see what they were like.

June 1944

Always Remember !

*CARELESS WORDS CAN BE FITTED TOGETHER
BY SPIES TO REVEAL MORE THAN
YOU MEAN TO TELL.*

Washington, D. C.

To: ALL Returning Personnel.

The war goes on and you're still in it. *SPIES ARE EVERY-WHERE.* So remember, a careless word by yourself, your family or a friend may cost the lives of Americans thousands of miles away.

CARELESS WORDS ALREADY HAVE COST TOO MANY LIVES
Keep Military Secrets to Yourself.

GEORGE C. MARSHALL
Chief of Staff, U. S. Army

ERNEST J. KING
Commander-in-Chief, U. S. Fleet

(over)

24-51818ABCD

This card details the guidelines for censorship of mail during the War.

DON'T REVEAL THE FOLLOWING

DON'T tell the name of ships.

DON'T tell locations or names of airfields.

DON'T tell locations of organizations overseas.

DON'T tell the station or assignment of individuals.

DON'T discuss the size or routes of convoys.

DON'T discuss sailing points or destinations.

DON'T discuss airplane routes.

DON'T discuss our weapons or airplanes or tactics.

DON'T discuss instruments of any kind.

YOU MAY TALK OF THE FOLLOWING

You MAY mention the cities and places visited if they are generally known.

You MAY tell personal experiences if exact locations and the designation and size of units are not mentioned.

You MAY discuss anything seen in motion pictures, read in newspapers, or heard over the radio.

(over)

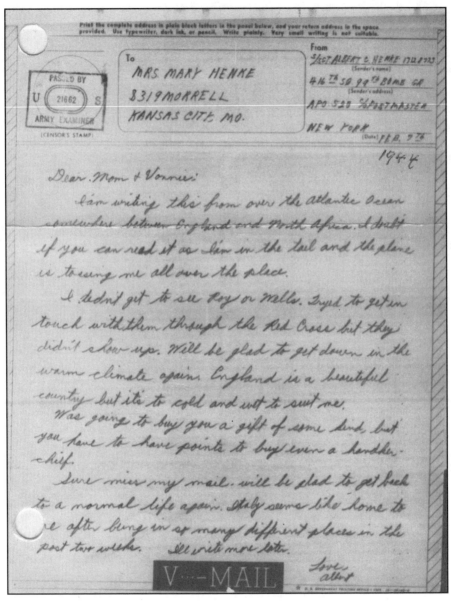

This is a V-Mail that was used to communicate with loved ones.

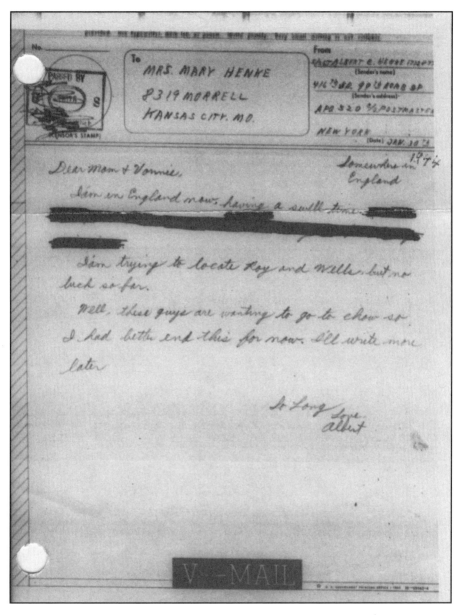

Sometimes V-Mails were censored to protect national security.

The positions that I manned on the B-17 Flying Fortress.

Chapter

The Trip Home

After completing my missions on April 2, 1944, I remained at the squadron, awaiting orders. I was not allowed to write home. My orders for the trip home did not arrive until April 17. I boarded a B-17 for a short hop from Foggia to Naples. I remember landing on a small airfield in Naples. This was a tight fit for a four-engine bomber. The next leg of our trip was by truck to the Replacement Depot located on the west side of Naples at the King's Race Track, a large concrete stadium. We spent 23 days waiting for a ship, dodging ack-ack. The stadium proved to be a great protection from the ack-ack guns. Weather permitting, once every morning, a lone photo plane would fly down from Rome at high altitude and check Naples Harbor for ships in or near the docks. We had action practically every night. Naples is approximately 125 miles south of Rome, and our forces were still on the Anzio Beachhead, and south of the Volturno River.

At last, on May 9, our shipping orders arrived. We boarded the liberty ship, USS William S. Few, by walking across gang planks laid over the sunken ships in the harbor. I thought it was a strange time of day, but we boarded the ship at 2:30 p.m. Later that night, we found out why. At 9:00 p.m. we sailed by the Isle of Capri. As we looked back toward Naples, we could see the Germans bombing where these ships had been earlier in the day. One was the ship we called home for 34 days. As we passed Capri and turned south, I felt, at last, we were on our way home!

However, I didn't realize the many sights and encounters we would meet before docking at New York Harbor.

The first day out, we headed for a point near Gela, Sicily. The ships were forming a convoy and waited until more ships coming north through the Suez Canal joined us. As we approached Sicily before daylight, we sailed past the Stromboli Volcano, which was erupting at the time. The red-hot lava was streaming down the side of the mountain into the Tyrrhenian Sea. What a magnificent sight!

As we continued on our journey, the convoy began to grow in size. We sailed on to Algiers, Algeria, and waited three more days for more ships to join us. (This was actually my third time to be in Algiers. The first time was in September, 1943, and then again when we flew General Joseph H. Atkinson to London, England, in January of 1944.) Approaching Algiers Harbor in the Mediterranean Sea, we noticed, from a distance, what looked like a dust storm. Instead of dust, it turned out to be a seventh-year locust plague. Swarms of insects, which resembled grasshoppers, covered the water in the harbor. I was told this swarm was flying from Spain and Portugal.

My final time in Algiers was quite an experience. (I still have the pass I used to go into Algiers. Written on the pass, dated May 22, 1944, was a notation, "My last day over seas.") I can say that I was in the famous Casbah. There, I noticed people sweeping the locusts up and storing them in bags. The natives considered these insects a rare delicacy. They prepared them in several ways; boiled in milk like stew, toasted, fried, or chocolate-coated. How would you like this cuisine served at your next dinner party?

On the last day in Algiers, as our ship pulled out of the harbor, approximately 30 large porpoises escorted our convoy out to sea. They followed us for miles, waiting for the ships to dump their garbage and sanitary tanks overboard. They were interesting to watch. Our ship sailed out to the Mediterranean Sea past the Strait of Gibraltar, and on to the Atlantic Ocean. By this time, our convoy increased to 170 ships.

We also had 12 destroyers that constantly encircled the armada until we reached New York Harbor.

Four days after we entered the Atlantic Ocean, heading due west to New York, we were under attack by a pack of German submarines. This experience convinced me that I would never make it as a sailor. I was assigned to sleep below deck. There were 500 men assigned to this area on rope hammocks stacked five deep. The ventilating system was not operating properly. It was impossible to sleep there, so many of us opted to sleep on the top deck. I decided this was the safest place to be, weather permitting, and I wore a life preserver day and night.

Our destroyers were kept busy launching depth charges. These charges would arch up into the sky, penetrate the surface of the water, and, after going down so many feet, would detonate, causing a concussion that created a loud bang against the ship below deck. I was never able to distinguish whether this blast was from the depth charges or from a U-Boat torpedo.

A day or so after the U-Boats left us, we sailed into a terrible storm that lasted for three days. Liberty ships are small vessels, and their construction could not compare to an ocean liner, so on high seas, they bounced around like corks. This same storm hit the European coast a day or so after the D-Day landing.

At approximately 1:00 a.m. on June 6, 1944, there was an announcement on the P.A. system, "The Allies are landing. The invasion is taking place!" THANK GOD D-Day finally arrived! I remember I was on the forward top hatch trying to sleep.

The final days of the trip were smooth sailing. As we approached New York City, we could see the skyscrapers from way out at sea, and before we knew it, we were passing the Statue of Liberty. What a beautiful lady! We docked at Pier 57, next to the ill-fated liner, the Normandy, that had burned and was lying on her side at the dock next to ours. There was an announcement over the P.A. system as we docked, "Everyone pick up your gear and prepare to disembark." That was an order we complied with in a hurry.

When we came down the gangplank, some women from the Red Cross handed each of us donuts and a full quart of milk. This was the first milk I had had since leaving the States. I'll never forget how good it tasted. Next, we boarded a ferry and crossed the harbor to New Jersey. We then traveled by truck to Camp Kilmer. Upon our arrival, we were served a steak dinner and were told that if everyone cooperated, processing would be completed and we would be on our way home by noon the next day. In my case, this was to Jefferson Barracks, St. Louis, Missouri.

At Jefferson Barracks, I received a 21-day delay- in- route. This was my first furlough since enlistment. After the furlough, I was to report to the Kansas City Union Station, to board the "Florida Special" train to Miami Beach, Florida, for two weeks at the Atlantic Towers for R and R (Rest and Relaxation).

When I reached St. Louis, I decided to go to Newport, Arkansas, where my brother, Harold was stationed. Harold was commanding officer of a basic flying school there, and we had not seen each other since he enlisted in December of 1941. Harold had our Pontiac with him at the base and I thought I would need the car when I got home. When I arrived at Newport, it was late at night so I got a hotel room and called the base and left a message for him to call me. I did not say who I was, and Harold thought the message was from one of his men who needed some help. So instead of calling me, he came to the hotel and was floored when I opened the door. Harold said he was in line for a furlough and if I could wait a day or two so he could make arrangements, we could go home together. I had not called Mom or Bonnie to tell them I was in the States, so we decided it would be fun to just surprise them. As soon as Harold was able to go, we took off for home (Kansas City). It was probably around midnight when we finally arrived. Mom and Bonnie were asleep. I'll never forget the look on their faces when they answered the door…Gee, it was great to be home!

The liberty ship, USS William S. Few, brought us over rough seas back to the U.S.A.

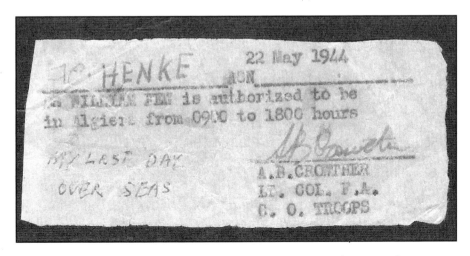

This is the actual pass (dated May 22, 1944) I used to go into Algiers—my last day overseas.

Upon completing my 50 missions, this photo was taken for squadron records.

My brother, Captain Harold W. Henke, and myself, Staff
Sergeant Albert C. Henke, dressed in Army uniforms.

Harold, Mom, Bonnie, and I at our house in Kansas City, Missouri.

Chapter

Home at Last

It was so good to be home. We crammed as much as we could into those 21 days. Mom, Bonnie, Harold, and I were so happy that the family could be together again. Harold and I visited with many of our friends and neighbors. Most of our friends who were our age were in the service, but we found out how they were and what they were doing. We went to Brunswick, Missouri, to visit our uncles and their families.

Harold and I went to Western Auto, too. There were many new faces, but many of the department heads were still there. They really treated us royally. We will never forget that the tire buyer arranged for us to get a set of tires for our car, which we desperately needed. (Gas rationing and tire rationing were in effect at this time and it was practically impossible to get gas or tires unless you worked for a defense plant or your job was considered important to the War effort. Unfortunately, Uncle Sam did not think a car was needed by servicemen.) We were also lucky that our local gas station attendant gave us some gas stamps. He said that some of his customers received more stamps than they could use so they gave them to him to give to people who needed them.

I also was able to tour the Pratt-Whitney Defense Plant south of Kansas City, where my relatives, Rosetta Bondy and Jack Barnhardt, worked. Pratt-Whitney manufactured airplane parts for military aircraft, and this is where some of the B-17 Flying Fortress engines were produced.

When our furlough ended, Harold drove the Pontiac back to Arkansas, and I boarded the Florida Special at Union Station for Miami, Florida. My orders were for two weeks of rest and relaxation at the Miami Towers hotel. After I unpacked my gear, I decided to take a walk on the beach. I couldn't believe my eyes, when I looked up and walking toward me was none other than Dan Ives. He had arrived there that same day. We decided that the Air Force was never going to split us up. However, this was the last time, while in service, that we were together. Dan received orders to go somewhere in South Dakota, and mine were to Pyote, Texas. I looked on maps but couldn't find Pyote, Texas, listed. I ended up going to AAA and they found it on one of their maps. It was 70 miles south and west of Midland, Texas, where I took basic training. It seemed that I could never get away from Texas.

Harold had contacted me previously and said he had been transferred to Cochran Field at Macon, Georgia. He had purchased a 1940 Chrysler and wanted me to come by his base and pick up the Pontiac.

After leaving Harold's base at Macon, Georgia, I began my trip to Rattlesnake Army Base at Pyote, Texas. I noticed from the map that I received from AAA that I would be going very close to Caney, Kansas. This was Vernon Wells' hometown. His folks had written to me quite often while I was overseas. I decided I had a little extra time before I had to report for duty in Texas, and this would be a good opportunity to meet them.

I thought I would visit with them and then drive to Wichita to spend the night. They seemed happy to meet me, and they treated me like I was part of their family. They insisted that I stay overnight with them, giving me the master bedroom (a far cry from the tents in North Africa!). I really enjoyed visiting with them, and it was a welcome break in the long trip to Texas.

I drove the Pontiac to the Rattlesnake Army Air Base, near Pyote, Texas. This was a B-29 base. I had a letter of recommendation from Major Morris to apply for pilot training, and I had been accepted. However, in the first week I was there, I saw two B-29s explode for no apparent reason. The B-29 was a new plane, the first plane to have pressurized cabins. The engineers were still working the bugs, out of them. Sometimes, if there was a spark from the engines, it would cause the oxygen to explode. The next day, after I saw the second one explode, I went to the commanding officer and asked that my name be removed from the pilot training list. He said he understood and put me in charge of an armament shop on the gunnery range. I remained in that position until the War was over.

A lot of servicemen were being discharged after the War in Europe ended. Discharge was done according to the point system in which your time in the service, combat duty, etc. counted as so many points. I had more than three times the number of points to be discharged, but because I had been trained in central fire control, I was not eligible to be discharged. Three days after the fall of Japan, my discharge papers came through and I was headed home. Phillip Arnone, who was in charge of shipping at headquarters, came by my barracks that night. He said, "I noticed that you have private conveyance. Providing I can ride home to Kansas City, Missouri, with you, I will get our papers in order tonight, and we could leave for home early the next morning." I drove 1,050 miles in 27 hours, and we arrived in Kansas City, two days before we were to report to Fort Leavenworth for our discharge on September 12, 1945.

I spent a few days at home, and then went to Western Auto. They told me I would have a job when I got out of service. I wasn't sure that this was what I wanted to do because the government was offering new programs every day for returning servicemen. Western Auto also was offering better benefits now than when I had gone into the service. I didn't know if I wanted to go to college on the GI Bill or perhaps go to work for the Postal Service. Western Auto was in the process of starting a profit-sharing and pension plan that sounded pretty good, especially since I had (including my time in service) more than 5 years seniority and would be eligible for their plan immediately. I accepted a position as a buyer in the Supply and Equipment Department. This job entailed purchasing all of the supplies and equipment for the company stores, the associate stores, and warehouses for the nationwide company. The company was in the process of opening a lot of new stores. During the War, many of the manufacturing companies were producing items for the War effort and many items that were needed for new stores were not yet available. The first couple of years in this job were quite a challenge. Manufacturers were in the process of converting to peace-time production, and many items needed for the new stores were difficult and almost impossible to obtain. Everything was on backorder, which delayed the opening of many stores across the country. It was very frustrating.

The shortages also became very frustrating for the millions of returning servicemen who were anxious to begin their lives again. Building and plumbing materials, appliances, cars, and even men's clothing were difficult to find. (These guys were ready to pack those uniforms away and get back into civilian clothing.) Not only were many items difficult to find, the prices began to snowball, which caused the government to impose price controls on almost everything.

All I dreamed of during the War was getting a new car when I got home. I had saved money for a car while I was in the service. In order to get your name on a waiting list for a new car, you had to have a car to trade in (which few servicemen had, but I still had my Pontiac). Right after the War, car dealerships required a trade-in to get a new car. The reason for this was that they could make more money by selling the older cars because there were no price controls on trade-ins, and the profit was much higher. I don't remember how many months it took to get my new car, but I do remember how happy I was to have it. It was a 1946 Pontiac Streamliner.

In November of 1945, our department hired a new secretary, Mary Rose Haas. Mary was a secretary for me and several other guys in the department who also had just returned from the service. Western Auto really started to expand after the War and it became necessary for each of us guys to have his own secretary. I requested that Mary be my secretary and my wish was granted. I always liked Mary and thought of asking her out, but I thought there was too much age difference between us. In March, Mary had a birthday. It was then that I found out how old she was and found out there was less age difference than I thought (six years). I asked her out the next week. We went together for 18 months.

Mary lived in Shawnee, Kansas, which was a distance of about 23 miles from where I lived in Missouri. My brother, Harold (who by this time had also been released from the service and came back to work for Western Auto), told me no girl was worth driving that far to date. I thought this over and decided maybe he was right. So, I decided to ask Mary to marry me. Mary accepted. We were married at St. Joseph Catholic Church, in Shawnee, Kansas, on September 13, 1947. (Harold also married a "Western Auto Girl," Betty Bratton. They were married on October 1, 1949.)

When we were married, I moved "across the border" to Kansas, where we still live. We feel blessed to have had so many happy years together. This year (2007), we celebrated our 60th wedding anniversary.

We had four wonderful children, Nancy, Marsha, Don, and Sharon. We were blessed with five grandchildren.

Nancy lives in Indiana in a suburb of Chicago. She has two children, Julia and Michael Konopasek.

Marsha lives in Kansas with her husband, Pete Cahill, and their two children, Patrick and Kristi.

Don lives in Kansas with his wife, Kim, and their son, Wade.

Sharon married Paul Cahill (Yes, he is Pete's brother.), and they live "across the border" in Missouri.

I continued working for Western Auto and retired with 41 years of continuous service (which included the time I was in the Air Force). Harold also continued to work for Western Auto, and we both retired the same day. Shortly after we retired, the company started a senior overload program, where retirees could work part-time. Harold and Betty and Mary and I worked for another 19 years on this program. With the 41 years of continuous service and 19 years of part-time service, I worked for Western Auto 60 years. After we retired, and during the time we worked in the overload program, Harold and Betty and Mary and I traveled extensively across the United States. Many of our trips were to 99th Bomb Group Historical Society and other World War II reunions.

It was great to drive my 1940 Pontiac again.

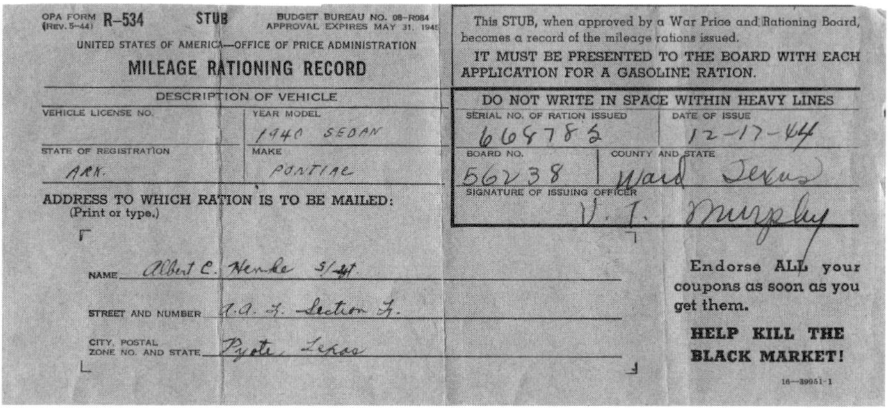
OPA FORM R-534 (REV. 5-44) STUB BUDGET BUREAU NO. 08-R084 APPROVAL EXPIRES MAY 31, 1945

UNITED STATES OF AMERICA—OFFICE OF PRICE ADMINISTRATION

MILEAGE RATIONING RECORD

This STUB, when approved by a War Price and Rationing Board, becomes a record of the mileage rations issued.

IT MUST BE PRESENTED TO THE BOARD WITH EACH APPLICATION FOR A GASOLINE RATION.

DESCRIPTION OF VEHICLE

VEHICLE LICENSE NO.	YEAR MODEL
	1940 SEDAN
STATE OF REGISTRATION	MAKE
ARK.	PONTIAC

DO NOT WRITE IN SPACE WITHIN HEAVY LINES

SERIAL NO. OF RATION ISSUED	DATE OF ISSUE
668785	12-17-44
BOARD NO.	COUNTY AND STATE
56238	Ward Texas

SIGNATURE OF ISSUING OFFICER V. T. Murphy

ADDRESS TO WHICH RATION IS TO BE MAILED:
(Print or type.)

NAME Albert C. Henke S/Sgt.

STREET AND NUMBER A.A.F. Section F.

CITY, POSTAL ZONE NO. AND STATE Pyote, Texas

Endorse ALL your coupons as soon as you get them.

HELP KILL THE BLACK MARKET!

16—39951-1

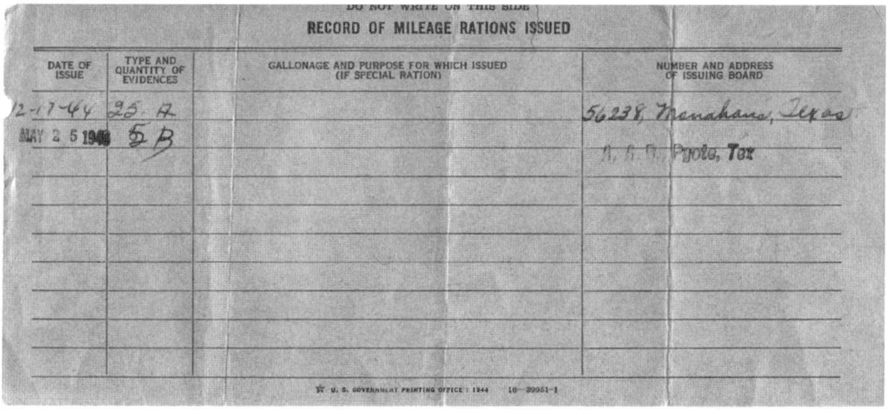
DO NOT WRITE ON THIS SIDE

RECORD OF MILEAGE RATIONS ISSUED

DATE OF ISSUE	TYPE AND QUANTITY OF EVIDENCES	GALLONAGE AND PURPOSE FOR WHICH ISSUED (IF SPECIAL RATION)	NUMBER AND ADDRESS OF ISSUING BOARD
12-17-44	25 A		56238, Monahans, Texas
MAY 2 5 1945	5 B		A. A. F. Pyote, Tex

U. S. GOVERNMENT PRINTING OFFICE : 1944 16—39951-1

Gas rationing was in effect during the War. We were fortunate to have extra gas rationing stamps to allow us to travel during our furlough.

This is me having a great vacation at the Miami Towers
Hotel in Miami, Florida. I was so surprised to run into
Dan Ives who was also sent there on furlough.

Pal of Sgt. Buddy Wells Visits War Hero's Parents in Caney

Although Mr. and Mrs. V. E. Wells have been anxiously awaiting the return of their son, S. Sgt. "Buddy" Wells from England and have been greatly disappointed because he has not been returned to the states after completing his bombing missions, they got the next best thing yesterday when Buddy's friend, S. Sgt. Albert Henke, of Kansas City stopped off here to visit them as he was en route to his home to spend a furlough.

Sgt. Henke and Sgt. Wells became buddies during their training days at Midland but they became separated upon going overseas, Henke being assigned to the Mediterranean war theater while Wells was based in England. But the two friends kept in touch with each other and since Sgt. Henke has returned to the states he has corresponded regularly with the Wells family.

Buddy and Albert met once earlier in the war when Buddy flew a mission to North Africa, and they had a grand visit. Since then both participated in many sky battles and young Wells is perhaps the most-decorated soldier to leave Caney.

Neither boy has been injured although each flew more than 50 combat missions. Sgt. Henke has made a souvenir of a piece of shell that would have penetrated his knee had it not struck a gun which he held between his knees.

Mr. and Mrs. Wells were most happy over the visit of young Henke as he gave them much information about their son and the things he has accomplished.

Mrs. Wells received a linen luncheon set from Buddy this morning as a belated birthday gift. He continues to be based in England and has served as an instructor since completing his combat missions.

I visited the Wells family in Caney, Kansas. They were excited to hear any information regarding their son, Bud (Vernon) Wells. I was treated like family.

ADVENTURES UNDER FIRE!

FOUR HUNDRED SIXTEENTH BOMBARDMENT SQUADRON (H)   JJM/ljt
NINETY NINTH BOMBARDMENT GROUP (H) ARMY AIR FORCES
Office of the Commanding Officer

10 April 1944.

SUBJECT: Letter of Recommendation

TO: Whom it May Concern.

    Staff Sergeant ALBERT C. HENKE, Air Corps
is making application for Aviation Cadet Training. Sergeant
Henke served as aerial gunner on a B-17 of which I was pilot
for a period of four months. On frequent combat missions
which I flew with him, I had opportunity to observe and appraise
his abilities. It was my observation that he performed his
duties, both on the ground and in the air, in a thoroughly
dependable, efficient and courteous manner. Sergeant Henke has
completed a successful combat tour of fifty missions over enemy
territory. Personally he is most engaging, his character un-
assailable and I have much pleasure in recommending him for
favorable consideration by those charged with selection of out-
standing individuals for Aviation Cadet Training.

JOHN J. MORRIS,
Major, Air Corps,
Commanding.

My letter of recommendation from Major John Morris, quali-
fied me for pilot's training. However, I decided not to
pursue a career in this field after I saw a couple of
planes crash on training missions.

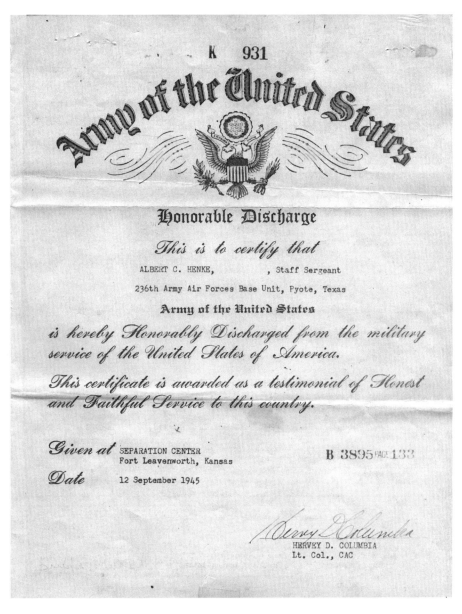

These are my Honorable Discharge papers from World War II.

fs

ENLISTED RECORD AND REPORT OF SEPARATION
HONORABLE DISCHARGE

1. LAST NAME - FIRST NAME - MIDDLE INITIAL	2. ARMY SERIAL NO.	3. GRADE	4. ARM OR SERVICE	5. COMPONENT
Henke Albert C		S Sgt	AAF	AUS

6. ORGANIZATION	7. DATE OF SEPARATION	8. PLACE OF SEPARATION
236th AAFBU Pyote Texas	12 Sep 45	Separation Center Fort Leavenworth Kansas

9. PERMANENT ADDRESS FOR MAILING PURPOSES	10. DATE OF BIRTH	11. PLACE OF BIRTH
8319 Morrell Ave Kansas City 3 Jackson County Missouri	1 Jul 1920	Brunswick Missouri

12. ADDRESS FROM WHICH EMPLOYMENT WILL BE SOUGHT	13. COLOR EYES	14. COLOR HAIR	15. HEIGHT	16. WEIGHT	17. NO. DEPEND.
See 9	Brown	Brown	5'7"	155 LBS.	0

18. RACE			19. MARITAL STATUS			20. U.S. CITIZEN		21. CIVILIAN OCCUPATION AND NO.
WHITE	NEGRO	OTHER (specify)	SINGLE	MARRIED	OTHER (specify)	YES	NO	
X				X		X		Clerk General 1-04.01

MILITARY HISTORY

22. DATE OF INDUCTION	23. DATE OF ENLISTMENT	24. DATE OF ENTRY INTO ACTIVE SERVICE	25. PLACE OF ENTRY INTO SERVICE
	6 Nov 42	6 Nov 42	Ft Leavenworth Kansas

SELECTIVE SERVICE DATA ►	26. REGISTERED		27. LOCAL S.S. BOARD NO.	28. COUNTY AND STATE	29. HOME ADDRESS AT TIME OF ENTRY INTO SERVICE
	YES	NO		Jackson Missouri	See 9
	X				

30. MILITARY OCCUPATIONAL SPECIALTY AND NO.	31. MILITARY QUALIFICATION AND DATE (i.e., infantry, aviation and marksmanship badges, etc.)
Airplane Armorer 911	Carbine Marksman 29 May 43

32. BATTLES AND CAMPAIGNS

GO 33 WD 45   Air Offensive Europe   Naples-Foggia   Rome-Arno

33. DECORATIONS AND CITATIONS

Good Conduct Medal   Air Medal with One Silver and Four Bronze Oak Leaf Clusters

34. WOUNDS RECEIVED IN ACTION

None

35.	LATEST IMMUNIZATION DATES			36.	SERVICE OUTSIDE CONTINENTAL U. S. AND RETURN		
SMALLPOX	TYPHOID	TETANUS	OTHER (specify)	DATE OF DEPARTURE	DESTINATION	DATE OF ARRIVAL	
6Dec43	11Nov43	4Jun44		14 Jul 43	E A M E T	21 Jul 43	

37.	TOTAL LENGTH OF SERVICE					38. HIGHEST GRADE HELD		
CONTINENTAL SERVICE			FOREIGN SERVICE				13 May 44	U S A	9 Jun 44
YEARS	MONTHS	DAYS	YEARS	MONTHS	DAYS		
1	11	11	0	10	26	S Sgt	

39. PRIOR SERVICE

None

40. REASON AND AUTHORITY FOR SEPARATION

Convenience of Government RR 1-1 (Demobilization)   15 Dec 44

41. SERVICE SCHOOLS ATTENDED	42. EDUCATION (Years)		
Aircraft Armament Course Buckley Field Colorado 1943	Grammar	High School	College
Flexible Gunnery Course Las Vegas Nevada 1943	8	4	0

PAY DATA

43. LONGEVITY FOR PAY PURPOSES			44. MUSTERING OUT PAY		45. SOLDIER DEPOSITS	46. TRAVEL PAY	47. TOTAL AMOUNT, NAME OF DISBURSING OFFICER
YEARS	MONTHS	DAYS	TOTAL	THIS PAYMENT			
2	10	7	$ 300.	$ 100.	None	$ 1.30	131.60
							LOYD R BEVINGTON
							Captain FD

INSURANCE NOTICE

IMPORTANT	IF PREMIUM IS NOT PAID WHEN DUE OR WITHIN THIRTY ONE DAYS THEREAFTER, INSURANCE WILL LAPSE. MAKE CHECKS OR MONEY ORDERS PAYABLE TO THE TREASURER OF THE U. S. AND FORWARD TO COLLECTIONS SUBDIVISION, VETERANS ADMINISTRATION, WASHINGTON 25, D. C.

48. KIND OF INSURANCE			49. HOW PAID		50. Effective Date of Allotment Discontinuance	51. Date of Next Premium Due (One month after 50)	52. PREMIUM DUE EACH MONTH	53.	INTENTION OF VETERAN TO
Nat. Serv.	U.S. Govt.	None	Allotment	Direct to V. A.				Continue	Continue Only	Discontinue
X			X		30 Sep 45	31 Oct 45	$ 3.30		$ 5 000	$ 5 000

54.		55. REMARKS (This space for completion of above items or entry of other items specified in W. D. Directives)
	RIGHT THUMB PRINT	Lapel button issued ASR Score (12 May 45) 106

56. SIGNATURE OF PERSON BEING SEPARATED	57. PERSONNEL OFFICER (Type name, grade and organization - signature)
Albert C. Henke	K D CLEVELAND Capt WAC Asst Adjutant KDCleveland

WD AGO FORM 53-55
1 November 1944

This form supersedes all previous editions of WD AGO Forms 53 and 55 for enlisted persons entitled to an Honorable Discharge, which will not be used after receipt of this revision.

I met Mary, my wife of 60 years, at Western Auto.
She was my secretary. I often joke that since the
company would not allow married couples to work for
the company, I married her to get rid of her. On the
other hand, she jokes that she married me so that
she could be the boss!

My 1946 black Streamliner Pontiac was one of the first cars produced after World War II. Since there were so few new cars like this one after the War, many people would stop to look at the car as I drove by. I was really proud of that car!

Mary and I were married September 13, 1947. We just celebrated our 60th wedding anniversary.

ADVENTURES UNDER FIRE!

This is a recent photo of our family. Front row (left to right): Patrick Cahill, Wade Henke, Michael Konopasek. Second row (left to right): Kristi Cahill, Albert Henke, Mary Henke, Julia Konopasek. Third row (left to right): Sharon Cahill, Kim Henke, Nancy Konopasek, Marsha Cahill. Fourth row (left to right): Paul Cahill, Don Henke, Pete Cahill.

Chapter

World War II Reunions

The focus of this chapter is on events related to my World War II experiences, in particular, those related to the 99th Bomb Group Historical Society Reunions and other related events.

The Rest of the Story

In the early 1980s, while on a trip to visit our daughter, Nancy, in Indiana, my wife, Mary, and I stopped to visit Clarence "Dan" Danielson, and his wife, Gloria. (Dan was the waist gunner on our crew.) They lived at Panorama Lake, Iowa, and had asked us to stop to see them and spend the night. I took along my 50-mission diary and some pictures of when we were overseas. Dan and Gloria were both interested in the diary. The next morning at breakfast, Gloria said she and Dan stayed up late to read the entire diary. She was especially interested in Mission #9, in which I told about a dead tail gunner in the plane next to ours. She told me that her first husband, John Thomas DeBaun, who was from Middletown, New York, was killed in action, probably on this same raid. He was a tail gunner on a B-17, flying out of North Africa. She said that she knows that he was killed on a raid over Weiner Neustadt, on that particular date. She said that she joined the WAACs (Women's Army Auxiliary Corps) soon after she received word of his death, and she did not receive any further information about him. However, she felt certain that the dead tail gunner that I referred to in my diary had to be her first husband. To quote radio commentator, Paul Harvey, "And now you know the rest of the story."

ADVENTURES UNDER FIRE!

Discovering the 99th Bomb Group
Historical Society

In the fall of 1983, I attended an air show at Richards-Gebaur Air Force Base, just south of Kansas City, Missouri. This air show featured some World War II airplanes. One of the airplanes featured in the show was a B-17. I had not been in a B-17 since I returned from overseas and wanted to see it. While touring the plane, I talked to the pilot, Jim Peters. I told Jim I had flown 50 missions in a B-17 in the 99th Bomb Group. He had also flown with the 99th and asked if I belonged to the 99th Bomb Group Historical Society. When I told him I hadn't heard of it, he gave me some information about the group. I joined the group soon after that. I also notified some of my friends, Dan Ives, Gene Canciglia, and Ross McKinney, who also joined.

This is my first visit with a B-17 as a civilian. It was at this time I discovered the existence of the 99th Bomb Group Historical Society.

My First 99th Bomb Group Reunion: Houston, Texas

In May of 1984, Dan Ives, his wife, Jean, my wife, Mary, and I attended our first reunion in Houston, Texas. This was a very interesting reunion. One of the highlights was a VIP tour of NASA. We were impressed. (Gene and Ross were not able to make it to this reunion, but were planning to attend future reunions.) Ives and I both took along pictures, etc., and I also took a typed version of my 50-mission diary. Colonel Faye R. Upthegrove, Commander of the 99th in 1942 and 1943, also attended this reunion. He was looking through the diary, and when he read about my first mission, he said, "That was my last mission on a B-17." (After completing his missions on the B-17s, he returned to the States and then came back to Italy with a B-24 outfit.) He told Dan and me that he was the pilot and led the group that day. Dan and I flew "Tail-End-Charlie." Dan flew ball turret position, and I flew the tail gun position. I told the Colonel about our lack of training, and he could hardly believe it. Ives said, "I can verify what Al wrote. We took our training together and neither of us had advanced training. This was the first time we were in a B-17." The Colonel said, "During that time, the U. S. Air Corp had a shortage of crews due to our heavy losses. Also, many of the original crews were completing their 50 missions and were being rotated back to the U.S. The need for replacement crews was a top priority."

This was the fourth reunion of the 99th Bomb Group. The four of us had a very enjoyable time and looked forward to future reunions. On our trip home from the reunion, we decided to stop at Colony, Kansas, to see Irel Green and his wife, Pearl. Dan and I took our gunnery school in Denver, Colorado, with Green, and Dan had not seen him since that time. I saw Green several times a year after the War when we went quail hunting together.

ADVENTURES UNDER FIRE!

My 50-mission diary was a topic of conversation at the reunion in Houston. (left to right) Dan Ives, Al Henke, Colonel Faye Upthegrove, and Colonel Wayne Thurman

Picture taken at Colony, Kansas (left to right): Jean Ives, Dan Ives, Irel Green, Al Henke and Pearl Green

My Second 99ᵗʰ Bomb Group Reunion: Seattle, Washington

My second reunion was the most memorable. It was held in July of 1985, in Seattle, Washington. Boeing hosted a party to help celebrate the 50ᵗʰ anniversary of the B-17. They invited anyone who had flown on a B-17. Our bomb group was well represented. At least 22 other bomb groups were also present. Boeing went all out to entertain us with an excellent air show and tours of planes. They served us a delicious lunch and hosted a wine- and cheese-tasting party in the afternoon, followed by a program featuring several World War II commanders.

Members of the Robert E. Lee crew, which included Gene Canciglia and his wife, Marjorie, and Ross McKinney and his wife, Martha, attended this reunion. We had such a nice visit and had so many memories to share. My brother, Harold, his wife, Betty, and their son, Kevin, accompanied us to this reunion. Harold joined the group as an associate member at this time. Many other friends attended, including Dan and Jean Ives.

When I met Ross McKinney, he said, "Al, there's someone here that you just have to meet." He introduced me to Clarence McGee. I last saw Lt. McGee when we were on the Regensburg raid on February 22, 1944. On this raid, six planes from the 416ᵗʰ left Foggia, Italy. Three planes returned early and only three of us continued on to the target. The planes that reached the target were our plane, piloted by Capt. Shaw, in the lead position, our right wing was Lt. McGee's plane, and George Perry was the pilot of the plane on our left. After we hit the target, McGee's plane went down over Augsburg, Germany. We did see three parachutes, but the plane was on fire, and we were not sure how many were able to get out. Through the years, I often wondered what happened to those other two crews. McGee said their crew survived, and they were taken prisoners of the Germans until the end of the War.

After the program at Boeing, as we were walking back to board our bus for the trip to our hotel, a fellow stopped Dan Ives and asked if the

99th on his hat meant that he was in the 99th Bomb Group. Ives answered, "Yes." The guy introduced himself as George Perry and said he was in the 99th until he had to ditch his plane in the Adriatic Sea after the Regensburg raid, on February 22, 1944. When Ives heard this he hollered at me. I couldn't believe it! Perry said he lived in Portland and decided he would come to the air show. I asked if it would be possible for him to come to the hotel where we were staying, because there was someone there I would like him to meet. It was quite a reunion for McGee, Perry, and me.

The last time I saw Perry was when his plane dropped out of formation. They were not far from Switzerland when this happened so our crew assumed that he had probably flown to Switzerland. However, that was not what happened. George said that they were shot up badly. They took a vote, and the whole crew wanted to try to make it back to the base. They threw everything they could overboard to try to lighten the load. They were doing quite well until it was necessary to transfer fuel. The fuel would not transfer, so they flew as far as they could and ended up ditching the plane in the Adriatic Sea. He said he decided to ditch the plane in the sea, so that the Germans could not repair it and use it against us. (Sometimes the Germans would repair these planes to flying condition, join our formation, and open fire on us.) The Germans rescued the crew from the sea, and they all ended up in prison camps until the end of the War.

I told Perry, I guess we were the lucky ones to make it back to base. However, our plane was hit by a rocket in the wing. The wing flopped all the way home. The rivets were pulled throughout the plane. It took an excellent pilot to fly under these conditions. Capt. Shaw, and his co-pilot, Captain John Morris, were two of the best! When we landed about an hour after the rest of the group, the plane was sent to the bone yard to be used for parts. It never flew again.

The 99th Bomb Group reunion was held in 1985 at Boeing Air-
craft Corporation in Seattle, Washington. (left to right)
Gene Canciglia, Al Henke, Dan Ives, J.J Cunningham, Joe
Kellerman, and Harold Henke (an assoicate member).

George Perry, Ross McKinney and Clarence McGee meet again for the first time after the Regensburg, Germany, raid of February 22, 1944.   Each feared that the others had been lost.

Other Reunions

We all looked forward to seeing each other at the reunions. The Canciglia's and McKinney's followed us home on several occasions and stayed a few days. We had our own little mini-reunions.

We also saw George Perry, and his wife, Dorothy, at many of the other reunions. His son lived in Springfield, Missouri, so they would fly into KCI airport, in Kansas City, Missouri, and spend a few days at our home before continuing on to Springfield. George spent his career as a high school teacher. He was interested in the memorabilia I had on World War II. For some reason, his personal effects were not returned to his family, when he became MIA (missing in action). George also wrote a book, *For You Der Var Iss Ofer*, about his time in service and his experiences at the prison camp. It is a very interesting book.

We attended almost every reunion until about 1995. (We had been scheduled to attend a reunion that year, when I had a heart attack and by-pass surgery, which I call my 51st mission!)

Harold, Betty, and
Kevin Henke

Gene and Marjorie Canciglia

ADVENTURES UNDER FIRE!

Dan and Jean Ives

Ross and Martha
McKinney

George and Dorothy Perry

Reunion of
Three World War II Theaters

Throughout the years after the War, Vernon "Bud" Wells and I kept in contact with each other. Wells lived in Northwest Indiana and worked as an engineer for U. S. Steel. When our daughter, Nancy, graduated from college, she accepted a job with Goodheart-Willcox Publishing Company, near Chicago and moved to Indiana. She lives just a short distance from the Wells family. We would see Bud and his wife, Doris, quite often when we visited Nancy. They treated Nancy like she was a member of their own family. Nancy referred to them as her, "Indiana Guardian Angels."

Several years ago, Nancy attended a book signing by Lt. Col. USAF (Ret.) Fred J. Olivi, for his book *Decision at Nagasaki—The Mission That Almost Failed*. Fred Olivi was the co-pilot of the B-29 aircraft that dropped the atomic bomb on Nagasaki, Japan. This ultimately caused Japan to surrender, thus bringing World War II to an end.

Nancy purchased books from Fred and told him that the books were for her two favorite World War II USAF veterans, Bud Wells and me. Fred wrote a note in each book, signed it, and told Nancy that he would like to meet the two of us. During our next visit to Indiana, Nancy invited Fred, Bud and Doris Wells, and Mary and me to dinner at Fred's favorite Italian restaurant, Giovanni's, in Munster, Indiana. Upon hearing that this was a special occasion and that we were World War II veterans, the owner of the restaurant, Nancy LoDuca, gave us the royal treatment from fine wine to a spectacular dessert tray!

It was an honor to meet Fred Olivi, a true World War II hero, and we all enjoyed the evening. We each served in a different theater during World War II. Fred was in the 20th Air Force in the Pacific Theater, Wells served with the 8th in the European Theater, and I was in the 15th in the Mediterranean Theater. I told Fred that just two days after Japan surrendered, my discharge papers came through and I headed for home to begin my civilian life again.

Vernon Wells and I met on many occasions over the years to reminisce about our World War II experiences.

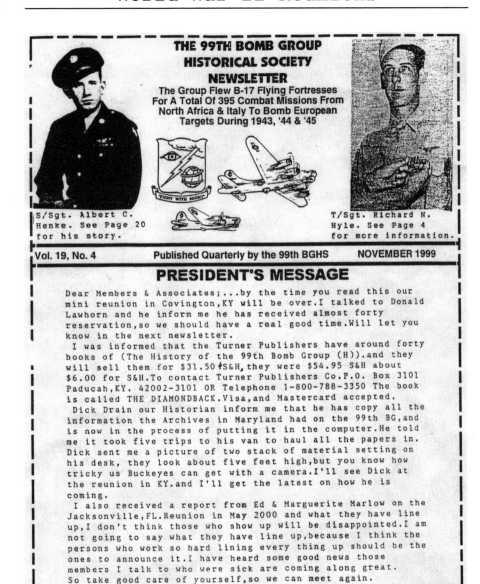

THE 99TH BOMB GROUP HISTORICAL SOCIETY NEWSLETTER

The Group Flew B-17 Flying Fortresses For A Total Of 395 Combat Missions From North Africa & Italy To Bomb European Targets During 1943, '44 & '45

S/Sgt. Albert C. Henke. See Page 20 for his story.

T/Sgt. Richard N. Hyle. See Page 4 for more information.

| Vol. 19, No. 4 | Published Quarterly by the 99th BGHS | NOVEMBER 1999 |

PRESIDENT'S MESSAGE

Dear Members & Associates;...by the time you read this our mini reunion in Covington,KY will be over.I talked to Donald Lawhorn and he inform me he has received almost forty reservation,so we should have a real good time.Will let you know in the next newsletter.

I was informed that the Turner Publishers have around forty books of (The History of the 99th Bomb Group (H)).and they will sell them for $31.50 +S&H, they were $54.95 S&H about $6.00 for S&H.To contact Turner Publishers Co.P.O. Box 3101 Paducah,KY. 42002-3101 OR Telephone 1-800-788-3350 The book is called THE DIAMONDBACK.Visa,and Mastercard accepted.

Dick Drain our Historian inform me that he has copy all the information the Archives in Maryland had on the 99th BG,and is now in the process of putting it in the computer.He told me it took five trips to his van to haul all the papers in. Dick sent me a picture of two stack of material setting on his desk, they look about five feet high,but you know how tricky us Buckeyes can get with a camera.I'll see Dick at the reunion in KY.and I'll get the latest on how he is coming.

I also received a report from Ed & Marguerite Marlow on the Jacksonville,FL.Reunion in May 2000 and what they have line up,I don't think those who show up will be disappointed.I am not going to say what they have line up,because I think the persons who work so hard lining every thing up should be the ones to announce it.I have heard some good news those members I talk to who were sick are coming along great. So take good care of yourself,so we can meet again.

Good Health

Robert J. Bacher Pres.

This is an example of the front page of a typical 99th Bomb Group Newsletter, used to keep members of the 99th Bomb Group Historical Society informed about events.

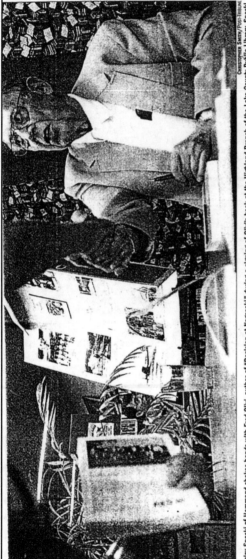

Stanley Speski of Hammond shakes hands with Fred Olivi, author of "Decision at Nagasaki," during a signing of Olivi's book at the Highland Branch of the Lake County Public Library. Speski built airstrips for B-29s in World War II and Olivi was former co-pilot of the plane that dropped the atomic bomb on Nagasaki during World War II.

Christopher Smith/Post-Tribune

Looking back at Nagasaki

Former pilot writes book about their WWII bomb drop over Japan

By Charles M. Bartholomew
Post-Tribune correspondent

HIGHLAND — "I wrote it because of all the distortions about what we did," said Lt. Col. U.S. Air Force (Ret.) Fred J. Olivi.

Olivi, former co-pilot of the plane that dropped the final, and largest, bomb of World War II on Japan, spent two hours at the Highland Public Library autographing his new book "Decision at Nagasaki: The Mission That Almost Failed."

Hanging in the air was the question to those who designed, built, and delivered the weapon that killed 45,000 people instantly:

How could you do what you did?

"The whole thing got a wrong slant — people thought we ended up in the crazy house. But we figured it was OK, because we saved American lives that would have been lost in the invasion of Japan," Olivi said.

The book details how the 11-man crew of "Bockscar" finally dropped the 22,000-kiloton plutonium bomb nicknamed "Fat Man" on their secondary target, despite a fuel system failure, after heavy clouds forced them to abandon their primary target.

Dyer's Guy Ausmus brought a balsa-and-paper model of the Enola Gay, which had bombed Hiroshima three days earlier, for Olivi to autograph. The model plane had

Please see NAGASAKI, Page B2

This article appeared in the Times Newspaper in Northwest Indiana on May 20, 2001. Following this original article is a clearer typed version.

FROM PAGE ONE

NAGASAKI

Continued from Page B1

a 52-inch wingspan.

"I built it over three years, using a lot of glue and X-acto knives. I've also got a P-38 and a P-47," he said, gingerly holding the fragile plane steady.

Olivi spent much time with fellow vets, often exchanging numbers to set up meetings or dinners.

To buy the book

Miles Books is located at 2618 Highway Ave. in Highland. The phone number is 838-8700.

John Torhon, 78, of East Chicago, was hospitalized on Okinawa in the summer of 1945.

"We could hear the B-29s taking off in the morning and then saw them coming back in the afternoon from bombing Japan," he said.

Many books were sold also for relatives and friends who were in the war. Two of the three books bought by war buffs Nancy Koropasek, 46, and her son Michael, 13, of Munster were for veterans.

"My Dad kept a diary with 50 missions that he flew as tailgunner on a Superfortress in Europe, and

A model of the Enola Gay built by Guy Ausmus sits on a table as people line up to have copies of "Decision at Nagasaki" signed by author Fred Olivi. Ausmus brought the plane to have it signed by Olivi.

we're trying to get him to write a book," Nancy said.

The most unusual war collector was Tony Ughetti, 33, of Hebron, who said, "Please don't think I'm gruesome" for saving pictures of mushroom clouds and old dosimeters, the badges worn by test person-

nel to measure radiation exposure.

But he had the most basic reason for coming to see Olivi: "Any time you can meet someone who changed history, it's a real treat."

James Roumbos of Miles Books in Highland said his store, which is now carrying the book exclusively,

will have a limited supply of signed copies at the publication price of $23.

Signing his last photo of the afternoon, Olivi concluded, "We hope that the two bombs that we dropped will be the only two ever dropped in war."

ADVENTURES UNDER FIRE!

Looking back at Nagasaki

Former pilot writes book about their WWII bomb drop over Japan

By Charles M. Bartholomew

Highland—"I wrote it because of all the distortions about what we did," said Lt. Col. US Air Force (Ret.) Fred J. Olivi.

Olivi, former co-pilot of the plane that dropped the final, and largest, bomb of World War II on Japan, spent two hours at the Highland Public Library autographing his new book, "Decision at Nagasaki: The Mission That Almost Failed."

Hanging in the air was the question to those who designed, built, and delivered the weapon that killed 45,000 people instantly.

How could you do what you did?

"The whole thing got a wrong slant – people thought we ended up in the crazy house. But we figured it was OK, because we saved American lives that would have been lost in the invasion of Japan," Olivi said.

The book details how the 11-man crew of "Bockscar" finally dropped the 22,000-kiloton plutonium bomb nicknamed "Fat Man" on their secondary target, despite a fuel system failure, after heavy clouds forced them to abandon their primary target.

Dyer's Guy Ausmus brought a balsa-and-paper model of the Enola Gay, which had bombed Hiroshima three days earlier, for Olivi to autograph. The model plane had a 52-inch wingspan.

"I built it over three years, using a lot of glue and X-acto knives. I've also got a P-38 and a P-47," he said, gingerly holding the fragile plane steady.

Olivi spent much time with fellow vets, often exchanging numbers to set up meetings or dinners.

John Torhon, 78 of East Chicago, was hospitalized on Okinawa in the summer of 1945.

"We could hear the B-29s taking off in the morning and then saw them coming back in the afternoon from bombing Japan," he said.

Many books were sold also for relatives and friends who were in the war. Two of the three books bought by war buffs Nancy Konopasek, 46, and her son Michael, 13, of Munster were for veterans.

"My Dad kept a diary with 50 missions that he flew as tail gunner on a Super fortress in Europe, and we're trying to get him to write a book," Nancy said.

The most unusual war collector was Tony Ughetti, 33, of Hebron, who said, "Please don't think I'm gruesome" for saving pictures of mushroom clouds and old dosimeters, the badges worn by test personnel to measure radiation exposure.

But he had the most basic reason for coming to see Olivi. "Any time you can meet someone who changed history, it's a real treat."

James Roumbos of Miles Books in Highland said his store, which is now carrying the book exclusively, will have a limited supply of signed copies at the publication price of $23.

Signing his last photo of the afternoon, Olivi concluded. "We hope that the two bombs that we dropped will be the only two ever dropped in war."

Three World War II veterans Al Henke, Fred Olivi, and Vernon Wells enjoy a memorable dinner.

I was interviewed at an air show in Kansas about my World War II experiences.

Chapter

Honors and Achievements

As I reflect on my adventures during World War II, I feel it was a great honor to have served my country, to have lived history, and above all, to have come to know some true American heroes. This final chapter describes some of the honors and achievements I have received as a result of my service during World War II.

Medals and Certificates

The medals and certificates I received are shown here (color version of all the medals are shown on the cover of the book.) Brief descriptions of the medals are also given.

United States Air Medal — Awarded for aerial combat.

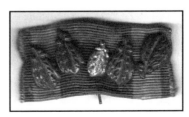

Close-up of oak leaf clusters on air medal. Each oak leaf cluster represents 10 combat missions.

Army Good Conduct Medal — Awarded for three years of good conduct service during World War II.

American Campaign Medal — Awarded for military service in the United States.

Victory Medal — Signifies the United States victory in World War II.

European-African — Middle Eastern Campaign Medal — Awarded for service in the Mediterranean Theater.

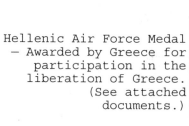

Hellenic Air Force Medal — Awarded by Greece for participation in the liberation of Greece. (See attached documents.)

AIR ATTACHE
EMBASSY OF GREECE
2228 MASSACHUSETTS AVE, N.W.
WASHINGTON, D.C. 20008
(202) 234-0561

June 25, 1966

Dear , Mr. Henke Albert C.

It is great pleasure and honour for me as a representative of the Hellenic Air Force to forward to you the Commemorative Metal on recognition of your Services during the period 1941-44 in Greece .

I take this opportunity to extend to you my warmest congratulations and best wishes .

Yours Sincerely

Colonel (HAF) George Foussekis
Air Attache

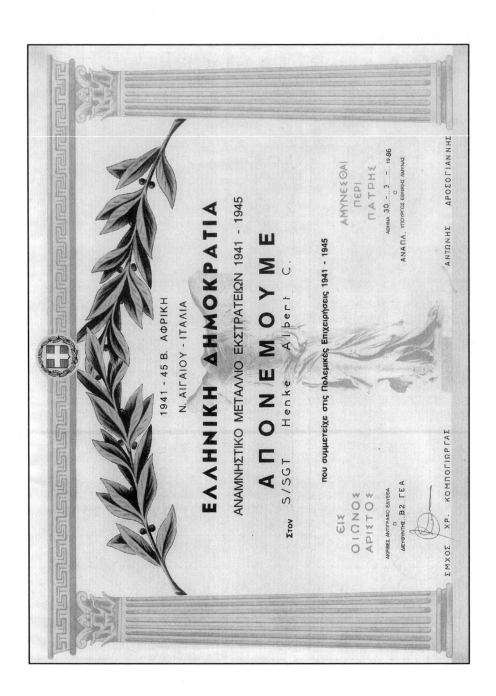

DEPARTMENT OF THE AIR FORCE
HEADQUARTERS UNITED STATES AIR FORCE
WASHINGTON 25, D. C.

2 May 1951

Mr. Albert C. Henke
8319 Morrell Avenue
Kansas City, Missouri

Dear Mr. Henke:

The Air Force takes pride in forwarding you a Certificate of
Valor conferred upon you by the Commanding General of the Air Forces
in the Mediterranean Theater of Operations in recognition of your
achievements in that theater during World War II.

This certificate does not constitute a basis for the award of
any decoration, but is proffered as tangible evidence of your significant contribution to the Air Forces in the Mediterranean Theater.

Sincerely,

JOHN McM. GULICK
Lt Colonel, USAF
Office, Director of Military Personnel

1 Incl
   Certificate

B4812

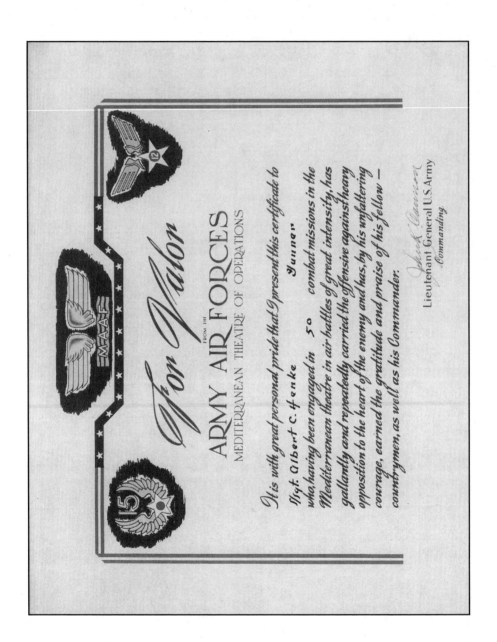

For Valor

ARMY AIR FORCES

FROM THE

MEDITERRANEAN THEATRE OF OPERATIONS

It is with great personal pride that I present this certificate to

S/Sgt. Albert C. Henke

Gunner

who, having been engaged in 50 combat missions in the Mediterranean theatre in air battles of great intensity, has gallantly and repeatedly carried the offensive against heavy opposition to the heart of the enemy and has, by his unfaltering courage, earned the gratitude and praise of his fellow – countrymen, as well as his Commander:

Lieutenant General U.S. Army

Commanding

Induction into the
Forest of Friendship:

The International Forest of Friendship, in Atchison Kansas, is a living tribute to the history of aviation and aerospace. It is dedicated to honoring those who have contributed to or are still contributing to all facets of aviation. Honorees are nominated and must be accepted by the Forest Committee. The names of the honorees are carved into granite plaques and embedded into the Memory Lane sidewalk that winds thought the Forest of Friendship. I was honored to be inducted into the Forest of Friendship on June 14, 1997. My Army buddy, Vernon Wells, was inducted one year later.

Fifty-two new names joining
Forest of Friendship path

Fifty-two individuals will be inducted into the Forest of Friendship this year. The 1997 honorees are:

Meigs Adams
Wendall Anschutz
Juanita Pritchard Bailey
Ray J. Baker
June Basile Bartelt
Diane Armour Bartels
Brig. Gen. Paul M. Bergman
Albert L. Bresnik
Marilyn (Mike) Seafield Browning
Mid Cassidy
Col. Clarence F. Cornish
Nancy Batson Crews
Faith (Faye) Douthitt
Lois A. Erickson
Albert C. Henke
Lu Curtis Hollander
Joan Hrubec
Woody Lesikar
Kelly Hamilton
John Jamgochian
Candalyn C. (Candi) Kubeck
Irene Lerverton
Betty MacGuire
Gay Dalby Maher
Joseph S. Marriott
Ellen Marie (Peggy) Mayo
Doris E. Miller
William W. Miller, M.D.
Jean Hanmer Pearson
Jan Perry
Kelly R. Petersen
John Piersma
Zyvonne D. Powell
Sarah Ratley
Sondra Ridgeway
Marion W. (Babe) Ruth
Walter M. Schirra, Jr.
Jacqueline Smith Scott
Carolyn S. Shoemaker
Eugene M. Shoemaker
Herb C. Sundmacher
Virginia Sutherland
Madeline (Mimi) Tompkins
Col. Roscoe Turner
LaVerne (Billie) Smith
Jean Roberts Wilson
Nancy Lucile Wright
Lucy B. Young
John Harold Ewert
Margaret Dorothy Jamieson Ewert
Ferdinand Graf von Zeppelin

This is the list of inductees who were honored on June 14, 1997, in Atchison, Kansas.

The International Forest Of Friendship
Atchison, Kansas

Albert C. Henke

has been honored

in

Memory Lane

in

The International Forest of Friendship

for

exceptional contributions to aviation.

M. Scott Knoch
Mayor, City of Atchison

Co-Chairman

Co-Chairman

June 21, 1997
Date

My certificate of induction into the Forest of Friendship.

Diary lands area man in Forest of Friendship

By Joyce Rabas
Sun Staff Writer

When Albert Henke sent his World War II flight diary to St. Joseph School with his daughter, Nancy, he could not have foreseen the result.

Nearly three decades later, the Shawnee resident has been inducted into the International Forest of Friendship in Atchison.

The Forest, a bicentennial project of the city of Atchison and the International 99s, serves as a living memorial to the world history of Aviation and Aerospace. It includes trees for each of the 50 states and 38 foreign countries.

"Every time they climbed into a plane, they didn't know if they'd come back," said Sister Phyllis Dye, who taught Nancy's sixth-grade class at St. Joseph's School. Dye nominated both Henke, who was a B-17 tail gunner, and Ray Baker, who was a B-17 navigator, for inclusion in the Forest. "When Nancy shared her father's diary with my class, I said he should write a book."

In fact, over the years several people have consulted Henke's diary as they wrote their own books, and Henke is currently polishing his first-hand accounts and impressions of his 50 bombing missions with the Army Air Force for publication.

Henke enlisted in 1942, and was originally assigned to the 12th Air Force. However, two months later the 15th Air Force was activated, and he was based in North Africa.

"These first 14 missions were especially long and dangerous," said Henke. That was because the bombers flew without fighter escort from Tunisia to Germany. "The sky was often black with flak, rockets and fighters."

One of his roughest missions took place on Feb. 22, 1944. Orders called for his squadron to bomb Hitler's Messerschmitt Aircraft Factory in Regensburg, Germany.

"Losses were extremely heavy that day," said Henke. "The Americans lost 52 bombers. Our crew was in a brand new B17G, and the damage to it was so severe this was the plane's first and last mission."

In the end, Henke's new plane was the only member of the 416th Squadron to make it to the target and limp back to the base.

The mission was later described by Major Gen. Nathan Twining as "the turning point of the air war in Europe."

WARTIME DIARY — Albert Henke of Shawnee kept a diary of his 50 bombing missions during World War II. The McAnany Estates resident is converting his firsthand accounts and impressions of the role the Army Air Force played in winning the air war in Europe into a book. Henke was recently inducted into the International Forest of Friendship memorial to the world history of aviation and aerospace in Atchison.

Sun Photo by Joyce Rabas

This article appeared in The Sun Newspaper in Shawnee, Kansas, on August 27, 1997. The following page features a clearer typed version of this original newspaper article.

Diary lands area man in Forest of Friendship

By Joyce Rabas
Sun Staff Writer

When Albert Henke sent his World War II flight diary to St. Joseph School with his daughter, Nancy, he could not have foreseen the result.

Nearly three decades later, the Shawnee resident has been inducted into the International Forest of Friendship in Atchison.

The Forest, a bicentennial project of the city of Atchison and the International 99s, serves as a living memorial to the world history of Aviation and Aerospace. It includes trees for each of the 50 states and 38 foreign countries.

"Every time they climbed into a plane, they didn't know if they'd come back," said Sister Phyllis Dye, who taught Nancy's sixth-grade class at St. Joseph's School. Dye nominated both Henke, who was a B-17 tail gunner, and Ray Baker, who was a B-17 navigator, for inclusion in the Forest. "When Nancy shared her father's diary with my class, I said he should write a book."

In fact, over the years several people have consulted Henke's diary as they wrote their own books, and Henke is currently publishing his first-hand accounts and impressions of his 50 bombing missions with the Army Air Force for publication.

Henke enlisted in 1942, and was originally assigned to the 12th Air Force. However, two months later the 15th Air Force was activated, and he was based in North Africa.

"These first 14 missions were especially long and dangerous," said Henke. That was because the bombers flew without fighter escort from Tunisia to Germany. "The sky was often black with flak, rockets and fighters."

One of his roughest missions took place on Feb. 22, 1944. Orders called for his squadron to bomb Hitler's Messerschmitt Aircraft Factory in Regensburg, Germany.

"Losses were extremely heavy that day," said Henke. "The Americans lost 52 bombers. Our crew was in a brand new B-17G, and the damage to it was so severe this was the plane's first and last mission."

In the end, Henke's new plane was the only member of the 416th Squadron to make it to the target and limp back to the base.

The mission was later described by Major Gen. Nathan Twining as "the turning point of the air war in Europe."

Honors and Achievements

My Army buddy, Vernon Wells, was inducted into the Forest of Friendship in 1998. Our plaques are near each other in the Italy section, on the Memory Lane sidewalk.

Grandpa's War Stories
by Michael Konopasek

He walks two miles every day,
And stops to chat along the way.

He knows a lot about World War II,
So much he could write a book or two.

He grew up in the Depression with the philosophy,
You must work for a living, because nothing comes free.

He worked at Western Auto's Home Office for 60 years,
Pricing bikes, refrigerators, car parts, and gears.

He married his secretary and had three girls and a boy,
Then five grandkids were added who he seems to enjoy.

I respect him as a hero and history buff.
He can tell you stories until you've had quite enough.

His stories are interesting beyond compare.
This man has more stories than pieces of hair.

He tells of fighting the Nazis and nations torn by war.
When he's finished, I find I'm left begging for more.

Whoever knew that a man so feeble and old,
Could have been so courageous, determined, and bold.

Although his battle wounds may never mend,
He is still my grandpa, storyteller, and friend.

My grandson, Michael Konopasek, wrote this poem for a class assignment at school. Although I'm proud of the poem, I take exception to the part about my being "feeble and old!" He'll be feeble and old someday, too.